D0803192

10159

45-

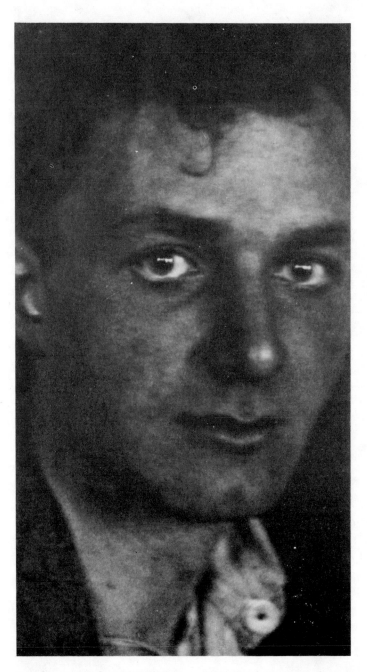

Stephen Spender, 1929 (Courtesy Humphrey Spender)

STEPHEN SPENDER

LETTERS TO CHRISTOPHER

Edited by Lee Bartlett

STEPHEN SPENDER'S LETTERS
TO CHRISTOPHER ISHERWOOD
1929–1939
With
"The Line of the Branch"–Two Thirties Journals

Black Sparrow Press – Santa Barbara – 1980

LETTERS TO CHRISTOPHER: STEPHEN SPENDER'S LETTERS TO CHRISTOPHER ISHERWOOD 1929-1939, With "The Line of the Branch"—Two Thirties Journals. Copyright © 1980 by Stephen Spender.

PREFACE Copyright © 1980 by Stephen Spender.

INTRODUCTION and NOTES Copyright © 1980 by Lee Bartlett.

All rights reserved. Printed in the United States of America. No part of this book may be used or reproduced in any manner whatsoever without written permission except in the case of brief quotations embodied in critical articles and reviews. For information address Black Sparrow Press, P.O. Box 3993, Santa Barbara, CA 93105.

The cover portrait of Stephen Spender is by Wyndham Lewis and is Copyright © by the Estate of the late G. A. Wyndham Lewis. It is used with their permission. Thanks is also due the City Museum and Art Gallery, Hanley, Stoke-on-Trent who kindly supplied a color slide of this oil painting which is in their possession.

Photographs courtesy of Humphrey Spender.

LIBRARY OF CONGRESS CATALOGING IN PUBLICATION DATA

Spender, Stephen, 1909-
   Letters to Christopher.
   Bibliography: p.
   Includes index.
   1. Spender, Stephen, 1909-   —Correspondence. 2. Isherwood, Christopher, 1904-   —Correspondence. 3. Authors, English—20th century —Correspondence. I. Isherwood, Christopher, 1904-   II. Bartlett, Lee, 1950-   III. Spender, Stephen, 1909-   Line of the branch. 1980. IV. Title.
PR6037.P47Z544 1980   821'.912 [B]   80-23513
ISBN 0-87685-470-6
ISBN 0-87685-471-4 (lim. ed.)
ISBN 0-87685-469-2 (pbk.)

Stephen Spender

Contents

Photographs follow page 68.

Preface

I first met Christopher Isherwood in Auden's rooms at Christ Church, Oxford, in 1928. Auden had already told me that Isherwood was The Novelist of the Future, and I could easily believe this. With his "squat spruce figure," his eyes which looked appraisingly at me and, above all, with his emphatic utterance, which incisively comprehended everything I stumblingly tried to explain about myself (my chief topic of conversation), I was completely on his side in what seemed a heroic battle of dramatic complexities of his life from the moment I first met him.

His appearance, with the eyes looking into all our futures, as though at some distant harbour; eyes wrinkled at the corners in a face at once boyish and with worried lines that reminded me of a sea captain. One imagined his hands on the tiller steering the ship to the North.

After Oxford, I met him several times in London. He told me of his ambitions as a novelist, which at that time were modelled on Turgenev: his life's work was to write a dozen brief but perfect novels. I visualized them in a row on a bookshelf behind him.

He left London and went to Berlin. From there he occasionally wrote brief letters and postcards to me, missives from the Front. Wherever he was seemed to me to be the trenches. When he asked me to join him in Berlin it was as though some admired commander had asked me to be his adjutant; and it was in this spirit that I joined him for months at a time through freezing Berlin winters and once or twice through Baltic summers on the island of Sellin.

As appears from the letters I wrote him, his patience with my hero-worship combined with my egotism wore thin, and after a couple of years I was no longer the colleague he wished with him in Berlin. Fundamentally, I think, what irritated him was my excessive adulation, my inability to keep myself at a critical distance from him I so admired, my gift for making those I loved feel guilty because of

9

the superfluity of my so often demonstrated generosity in attempting to buy reciprocal love. Together with this Christopher was a bit jealous of my beginning to have a life of my own. When out of attempted clumsy tactfulness I suggested to him that when I next returned to Berlin we should live more distanced lives, his irritation boiled over and he wrote me a letter which I did not have sufficient humour to take as a bit absurd, in which he declared that Berlin was not big enough for the two of us.

I destroyed this interesting document and was tremendously and tearfully hurt. However, we soon repaired the breach in our friendship which has continued uninterruptedly until the present day. But it was perhaps not entirely healed when we attempted to share a house, together with two friends (one of each of us) at Sintra in Portugal. The arrangement only lasted a few weeks.

Before this, when I decided to abandon Berlin (so soon to be taken over by Hitler) to Christopher, I went to Barcelona. My reasons for doing so throw light on my complete immaturity. Friends of mine in England (Harold Nicolson and Edward Sackville-West) had told me that in Barcelona there languished a neurotic, greatly oppressed and beautiful young German called Hellmut who needed above everything else in the world an English friend. I at once set out for Barcelona determined to fill this gap in Hellmut's life and to "cure" him of his neurosis. Within hours of my arriving there, I met him. He did not respond to the romantic feelings I had worked up about him, but he was rather touched at my continuing wish, nevertheless, to save him. He certainly was unhappy and oppressed, working for a German business man as a kind of butler and domestic servant. He felt perpetually humiliated by his employer (he had rather a genius for feeling humiliated). Although I had next to no money, I persuaded Hellmut to throw up his job, and to hike with me from Barcelona to Valencia, and that while I wrote poetry he would manage the house and be cured by my "love" for him.

During this journey I wrote a journal which gives a picture of the utter poverty of the South of Spain at this time and the xenophobia of Spaniards. As was inevitable, my arrangements with Hellmut collapsed. He went back not to Barcelona but to Berlin, where he sought out Christopher and complained to him bitterly about me. Christopher was at first impressed by these complaints, but very soon took the measure of Hellmut and his neurosis. Hellmut was genuinely unhappy, though he was not unloveable.

The above is, briefly, the background of my letters to Christopher over a period of some years. I am glad to say that in spite of their emotional ups and downs, they do reveal my admiration and love for the recipient, which has lasted more than half a century. Christopher's genius is to be entirely Christopher, and yet, at the same time to act out roles, as Chris, Mr. Issyvoo, and someone who calls himself "I," and this juggling of masks and personae has fascinated thousands of readers. It has also made him loyal and greatly entertained friends, of whom I count myself one of the most enduring.

Stephen Spender

Louisville, Kentucky
April, 1980

Introduction

IN THEIR PREFACE to *Oxford Poetry 1927*, W. H. Auden and C. Day Lewis wrote, "All genuine poetry is in a sense the formation of private spheres out of a public chaos."[1]* Yet for the English writers of *their* generation, what Samuel Hynes has called the *Auden Generation*, these "private spheres" were certainly connected by broad passageways, links which were both felt and cultivated. Auden, Day Lewis, and Stephen Spender were all at Oxford at more or less the same time, William Empson, John Lehmann, and Christopher Isherwood at Cambridge; all (save Isherwood the novelist) appeared in Michael Roberts' anthology of new poets, *New Signatures*, in 1931, and all remained to a greater or lesser extent in touch with each other throughout their lives, often collaborating and reviewing one another's books. As children, they all had lived through the trauma of the First World War, but were denied the chance for action and glory in the trenches. They emerged from adolescence with a sense of estrangement from history, worn-out, living in both a psychic and economic depression. "We were far too insular and preoccupied with ourselves," recalled Auden, "to know or care what was going on across the Channel. Revolution in Russia, inflation in Germany and Austria, Fascism in Italy, whatever fears or hopes they may have aroused in our elders, went unnoticed by us."[2] But they did notice, and they grew to care, so much so that what would come to distinguish this group of writers from that which had come into prominence in the twenties would be its intense political engagement. In his autobiography, *World Within World*, Stephen Spender would later write, "From 1931 onwards, in common with many other people, I felt hounded by external events."[3] The next ten years would see their private spheres shattered and re-assembled into a "generation" by the rise of Hitler, the Spanish Civil War, and a Second World War.

---

*Notes to the Introduction are on p. 19.

In his review of Samuel Hynes' seminal book on the English writers of the thirties, John Lehmann quipped that the subject "is rapidly becoming almost as fashionable as Bloomsbury."[4] That is Lehmann's wit, yet the past few years have witnessed an increasing number of memoirs, histories, critical books and articles, doctoral dissertations, novels (and the re-issuing of novels), films, and television documentaries about the period, culminating in 1976 with the publication of Hynes' *The Auden Generation* and Christopher Isherwood's *Christopher and His Kind*. This collection of letters from Stephen Spender to Christopher Isherwood is in one sense another hat thrown into that literary ring, although it is, I think, an important one. In 1929, Stephen Spender was twenty years old and an undergraduate at Oxford; Christopher Isherwood was twenty-four and had in November moved from London to Berlin. Both had published their first books the year before (though Spender privately and in a very small edition), but neither book had drawn much comment. During the next ten years, however, both young men would realize their vocations as writers, publishing between them a number of the generation's most important works: *Poems, The Destructive Element, The Still Centre, Mr. Norris Changes Trains, Goodbye to Berlin*, and others. By 1939, Stephen Spender would emerge as one of the generation's most prominent poets and essayists, Christopher Isherwood as a major novelist. In a very real sense, then, these sustained and sensitive letters from the naive "pupil" to the worldly-wise "master" written between those crucial years of 1929 and 1939, trace the evolution of one of the thirties' most significant literary friendships, against the backdrop of some of the most important social and political upheavals in modern history.

In editing the volume, it seemed to me that the letters rather naturally fell into three parts. The early letters, 1929-1931, though the most fragmentary and cryptic of the collection, give us glimpses of Spender's life as an Oxford undergraduate: a young writer's insecurities and his dissatisfaction with his early work ("I wish my poetry were better, I wish myself were maturer, so that I could fix the ideas instead of being overwhelmed by them when they come to me"); failed friendships and love-affairs; his essential loneliness there once Auden and Isherwood have left England ("Damn Oxford. When can one escape from such a place and live in peace?"). There is an early poem here, a fragment of another, and discussion of prose-in-progress. The section ends with a letter written after his leaving the university as Spender prepares to join Isherwood in Berlin: "How many years will it take before I can emerge from the waters at the point where you have emerged? It is though I had to *swim* that rotten Channel."

Part Two comprises letters written between 1932 and 1935, a period in which both Spender's experience and his reputation as a literary figure begin to widen. He has "swum" the Channel—the opening letters are accounts of his adventures in Barcelona ("certainly the most red hot revolutionary place I have ever been in"), while later ones trace his exploits in Vienna, Dubrovnik, and Innsbruck, as well as London. During these years, the poet's circle of literary acquaintances begins to widen, as he writes of meeting E. M. Forster and dining with Leonard and Virginia Woolf. Yet it is also a period of personal strife: he records the ending of one love affair and the beginning of another, his confusion over his sexual orientation, and fallings out (and reconciliations) with both Isherwood and John Lehmann. The role of the writer in the world is a growing concern, as Spender's aesthetics become more politicized:

> I can't write pretensions any more (or I don't want to) even when the pretensions are not mine but those of something like communism, which I believe in. I want to try and describe a phase of society with precision because when that phase is fully realized people will want to go on to what grows out of it. . . . I don't think poetry is useless because I think it can prepare people for political propaganda, and shake their prejudices.
>
> (Letter 14)

For Spender, these are the years of the publication of his first major book of poetry (*Poems*) and his first major book of prose (*The Destructive Element*), as well as his work on his first collection of published fiction (*The Burning Cactus*); for Isherwood, this period marks the publication of both *The Memorial* and *Mr. Norris Changes Trains*, as well as his collaboration with Auden on the first of their plays, *The Dog Beneath the Skin*. All these works are discussed here at some length by Spender. And as with Part One, there are drafts of poems (including a version of "New Year" which differs slightly from the published one, and previously unpublished selections from a "chorus" to *Vienna*), as well as detailed accounts of plans to turn his

15

long poem *Vienna* into a play and revisions for his unpublished novel, *The Temple*.

The final section includes letters written between 1936 and 1939, from Barcelona, Delphi, Vienna, Salzburg, Gibraltar, Suffolk, and London. Spender's literary reputation has become secure, as has Isherwood's, and with his work on *Forward From Liberalism* he has become progressively more active in public life:

> It is true that I am rapidly enlisting myself as one of what Nevinson calls the great 'stage army of the good' who turn up at every political meeting and travel about the country giving little talks, subscribe to things, do free articles, etc.
>
> (Letter 25)

Forward From Liberalism is chosen as a selection by the New Left Book Club, Spender writes for *Left Review*, and when the war in Spain erupts in full force, he writes of leaving "for 14 days on a rather important job to the rebel part of Spain." In his personal life, these letters trace the sundering of a major male friendship over his decision to marry Inez Pearn, and then finally his despair when in 1939 she leaves him. During this period, Spender's major literary endeavor is his play, *Trial of a Judge*, while Isherwood's are his collaboration on *The Ascent of F6* with Auden and the fiction which will go to make up *Goodbye to Berlin;* these are subjects here. Spender discusses the work of Aldous Huxley, Rosamond Lehmann, Garcia Lorca (whom he is translating), and in an enclosure to Auden, "Tom Eliot's" *Collected Poems* ("Perhaps Yeats, Laura Riding, and even Blunden can do this kind of pseudo-philosophic writing better"). As with the previous two sections, Spender also makes reference to poems in progress (which will be collected in his first volume of poetry since 1933, *The Still Centre*, in 1939), and includes a draft of "Hölderlin's Old Age" and a fragment of a Lorca translation.

Although in the early stages of this project I spent an afternoon at the home of Christopher Isherwood looking through the original letters, in preparing the manuscript I worked from Xerox copies which Mr. Isherwood kindly provided. For the few letters which were typewritten, this posed no problems; the bulk of the letters, however, were written in Spender's sometimes almost illegible hand, and the fact of the Xerox only added to the difficulty of the transcription. Still,

I have made every effort to insure accuracy, and accept full responsibility for any errors which a better eye may someday catch.

As for dating, Christopher Isherwood noted in his autobiography that many of his contemporaries neglected to date their letters, feeling perhaps that it was somehow beneath them as artists. Whatever his motivation, Stephen Spender was no exception. Many of the early letters have no date at all, while later ones indicate day and month, but not the year. As the envelopes have been lost, the problem in ordering the text is obvious. Fortunately, most of the letters contain internal evidence which makes dating possible; also, though memory is certainly not infallible, Mr. Isherwood dated them by year to the best of his recollection. Except in the case of obvious errors, I have accepted his informed guesses.

Many letters surely have been lost. In *World Within World*, Spender mentions that in 1930 he wrote numerous letters to Isherwood "the polar explorer" (p. 126); we have only five from that year, and just one from each of the next two—certainly Spender wrote more. Likewise, Isherwood retains no letters from 1938, and only one letter (albeit a major one) from 1939; again it is obvious that Spender wrote others. Often texts of enclosed drafts of poems and prose are mentioned, but many of these also have been lost. Luckily, the bulk of the correspondence seems intact, however.

In his article, "Editing the Letters of Letter Writers," Robert Halsband argues that the only *exact* text of a letter can be the manuscript itself. "Even if we used a photo-process," he writes, "we should then begin to worry about the color of the ink, the quality of the paper, the manner of folding the sheet and so on. When we decide to reproduce it by means of typography, we have made a great concession, and once having made it we need not be stingy as to its extent."[5] Following this principle, I have envisioned my task to be the production of as readable a text as possible, though without any substantive alterations. Errors in spelling have been silently corrected, while punctuation has been emended to conform to American standards. Occasionally I have supplied proper nouns or proper names in square brackets for clarification; Spender did not always underline titles, though here all are italicized. Whenever a passage of any substance is deleted in the original, or when there are marginal comments, this information is indicated in the annotations.

17

Finally, in a project of this kind one of the most crucial questions facing an editor is the nature and the extent of the annotations. For some readers, annotations are often distracting and needless; for others, they provide a sense of orientation and continuity. Here, my policy (aside from the treatment of deletions and marginal notes as mentioned above) has simply been to trust my own judgement, and I have used the annotations to explain cryptic or obscure references, literary references, and essential bits of history and biography. Along these lines, identification of many persons mentioned in the text is included in a list of "Major Figures in the Letters" following this introduction, rather than in the annotations themselves. Also, the letters in each section are preceeded by brief prefaces which attempt to place them in context.

As a proviso for permission to publish his letters to Christopher Isherwood and his thirties Journals, Stephen Spender retained the right to examine the final manuscript of this text and make any excisions he felt necessary to protect the interests of friends still living. He has exercised his option, though to a very limited extent. Occasionally he has cut a few lines (or, in a few instances, a passage), and in two or three cases he has supplanted a name with an initial. As the excised material is in all cases of an extremely personal nature, Spender's deletions in no way affect either the historical or critical value of the manuscript as we have it here; the effect of the cuts is, in short, negligible. I have indicated excisions with ellipses. In addition, Spender has sometimes added a word or a phrase for clarification; these additions have been enclosed in brackets.

In preparation of this text, four books were extremely useful: Spender's autobiography *World Within World* (published by Hamish Hamilton, 1951), Isherwood's *Christopher and His Kind* (published by Farrar, Straus and Giroux, 1976), Samuel Hynes' *The Auden Generation* (published by Viking Press, 1976), and H. B. Kulkarni's *Stephen Spender: An Annotated Bibliography* (published by Garland Publishing, 1975). I wish to thank both the authors and the publishers for allowing me to quote from them.

By way of acknowledgements, thanks go first of all to Stephen Spender, who on the way to the airport one fine California spring afternoon mentioned the existence of these letters to me, and who later allowed their compilation. Christopher Isherwood owns the originals, and he not only let me examine them, but kindly spent many hours ordering them for me at a time when he was deeply engrossed in the production of one of his own plays. To him I am also very grateful. I would also like to thank the helpful staff at the Bancroft Library, University of California at Berkeley, where the originals of the two Journals by Stephen Spender are located. Charles Monteith of Faber and Faber made some useful comments on an early draft. James Woodress, of the University of California at Davis, gave much support and advice, and as Graduate Chairman made it possible for me to spend a year teaching at the University of Bordeaux, where most of the work was done. Michael J. Hoffman and Karl Shapiro read the manuscript and were more than encouraging. I wish also to thank John Martin of Black Sparrow Press for his patience and interest, and Seamus Cooney for some last-minute suggestions. Finally, thanks go especially to my wife Mary for allowing me to spend a large part of a year in France at the typewriter. No small sacrifice.

Lee Bartlett

Bordeaux—Davis
April, 1980

[1] W. H. Auden and C. Day Lewis, eds., *Oxford Poetry 1927* (Oxford: Basil Blackwell, 1927), p. v.

[2] W. H. Auden, "As It Seemed to Us," *The New Yorker*, 41 (April 3, 1965), p. 180.

[3] Stephen Spender, *World Within World* (London: Hamish Hamilton, 1951), p. 137.

[4] John Lehmann's review appeared in the *Sunday Telegraph*; this passage was excerpted as a dust-jacket blurb for *The Auden Generation*.

[5] Robert Halsband, "Editing the Letters of Letter Writers," *Studies in Bibliography*, 9, 1958, p. 30.

The Major Figures in the Letters

AUDEN, W. H.: Poet, dramatist, essayist. Attended Oxford 1925-1928, where he met Spender (who hand-printed his first volume, *Poems*). Collaborated with Isherwood on the plays *The Ascent of F6* and *The Dog Beneath the Skin*, as well as *Journey to a War*, a travel book about China, during the thirties.

CROSSMAN, RICHARD: Spender and Crossman met at Oxford, where Crossman was a Fellow and Tutor from 1930 to 1937. From 1938 to 1955, he was Assistant Editor of *The New Statesman and Nation*, a journal which published a large number of Spender's articles, reviews and poems. In 1949, Crossman edited *The God That Failed*, which included Spender's accounts of his rejection of Communism in the late thirties.

EWART, GAVIN: Poet and critic. Educated at Cambridge, his *Poems and Songs* appeared in 1939.

FORSTER, E. M.: Novelist and essayist. In his autobiography *CaHK*,* Isherwood described Forster as his "master." Isherwood and Forster met through William Plomer, who in turn had been introduced to Isherwood by Spender.

GARDINER, MURIEL: Named "Elizabeth" in *WWW*, Muriel Gardiner met Spender in Mlini in the spring of 1934, and they were for a time lovers. In the mid-thirties, she was active in a group of Austrian Socialists, providing money for propaganda and political refugees.

HAMILTON, GERALD: Isherwood met Gerald Hamilton in the winter of 1930-31, when Hamilton was the sales representative for the London *Times* in Germany, and later introduced him to Spender. Hamilton was Isherwood's model for the character of Mr. Arthur Norris in *Mr. Norris Changes Trains*.

HEARD, GERALD: Essayist, philosopher. During the thirties, Heard published a number of works including *The Social Substance of Religion, The Emergence of Man*, and *The Third Morality*. Like Auden and Isherwood, he left England for America in the late thirties and settled, like Isherwood, in Southern California.

---

* Abbreviations: *CaHK, Christopher and His Kind; LS, Lions and Shadows; WWW, World Within World*.

HEINZ: Isherwood's German companion from 1932 to 1937. Introduced by Francis Turville-Petre, Isherwood "had no hesitation in falling in love with Heinz. It seemed most natural to him that they two should be drawn together. Heinz had found his elder brother; Christopher had found someone emotionally innocent, entirely vulnerable and uncritical, whom he could protect and cherish as his very own" (*CaHK*, p. 91).

HELLMUT: Spender's German companion on his trip to Spain, during the winter of 1932-33. He appears in Spender's short story "The Burning Cactus."

HYNDMAN, TONY: Called Jimmy Younger in both *WWW* and *CaHK*. Spender met Tony in 1933, and soon after hired him as his secretary. The two became lovers, and remained companions until Spender's marriage to Inez Pearn in 1936.

LEHMANN, JOHN: Editor, poet, essayist. Educated at Cambridge. Lehmann was managing the Hogarth Press when it accepted Isherwood's second novel, *The Memorial*, for publication. A close friend of both Spender and Isherwood, Lehmann published much of their writing in his *New Writing*, an influential left-wing journal which first appeared in the spring of 1936.

LEHMANN, ROSAMOND: Novelist. Spender met John Lehmann's sister Rosamond while he was an undergraduate. With her husband Wogan Philipps, she introduced Spender to the "civilised world of people who lived in country houses" with "their paintings and drawings of the modern French school, and a Roger Fry, Vanessa Bell, or Duncan Grant" (*WWW*, p. 144).

LEWIS, C. DAY: Poet and critic. Spender and Day Lewis met at Oxford through Auden. Co-editor of *Oxford Poetry 1927* with Auden. In 1929 he published *Transitional Poem*, in 1933 *The Magnetic Mountain*, and in 1935 his *Collected Poems*.

MANGEOT, OLIVE: Portrayed as Madame Cheuret in *LS*, and as both Margaret Lanwin and Mary Scriven in *The Memorial* by Isherwood. She was a Communist and "provided a club for Isherwood and his friends to which he brought nearly all his new acquaintances" (*CaHK*, p. 101).

"MARSTON": An Oxford undergraduate with whom, during his first years at the university, Spender was infatuated. A number of Spender's early poems are addressed to "Marston."

PEARN, INEZ: Spender's first wife. Married in late 1936, they separated in 1939. Spender's *The Still Centre* is dedicated to her.

PLOMER, WILLIAM: Poet and novelist. In 1929, Plomer, a South African, left his country and settled in England. Spender met him while working as secretary for the Oxford English Club in 1930.

READ, HERBERT: Poet, critic, publisher. During the thirties he edited *The Burlington Magazine*. One of Spender's sympathetic reviewers, his own *Collected Essays in Literary Criticism* was published in 1938.

SOLOWEITSCHIK, GISA: Spender met Gisa Soloweitschik on a skiing trip in Switzerland when he was an undergraduate and she was seventeen. He introduced her to Isherwood who "soon found out that there was an Oriental sense of untouchability in Gisa. . . . The result of the conflict was that although Gisa and Christopher were always at one another's throats, within a few weeks he knew her better than I had done in several years" (*WWW*, p. 128). Gisa formed the basis for Natalia Landauer in Isherwood's *Goodbye to Berlin*.

SPENDER, HUMPHREY: Stephen Spender's youngest brother. For a time, in 1939, he and his wife shared a house in Suffolk with Stephen and Inez.

SPENDER, MICHAEL: Stephen Spender's eldest brother. A scientist, he required of Stephen that he "should play a mythological role in his world of pure reason. He wanted me to be the Caliban to his Prospero, not because he envied me, but since, because I represented certain subjective attitudes, I served his scientifically rational universe by playing this grotesque part" (*WWW*, p. 46).

TURVILLE-PETRE, FRANCIS: Nicknamed "Fronny" by Isherwood and Auden, Turville-Petre appears in Isherwood's *Down There on a Visit* as Ambrose: "His figure was slim and erect and there was a boyishness in his quick movements. But his dark-skinned face was quite shockingly lined, as if Life had mauled him with its claws." Auden introduced Fronny to Isherwood, and Isherwood later introduced him to Spender.

WOOLF, LEONARD: Historian, critic, publisher of the Hogarth Press. Educated at Cambridge, he and Virginia Woolf published Michael Roberts' two anthologies, *New Country* and *New Signatures*, as well as Isherwood's *Mr. Norris Changes Trains*, *Lions and Shadows*, and *Goodbye to Berlin*.

WORSLEY, CUTHBERT: Friend of Stephen Spender's who went with him to Spain in an attempt to get information on the sinking of the Russian Ship *Comsomol*. Spender appears as Martin in Worsley's novel *Fellow Travellers*.

LETTERS TO CHRISTOPHER

PART ONE

1929–1931

When Stephen Spender first entered Oxford University, he recalled later in his autobiography, he felt like an outsider, "a new boy among public-school boys," whose interest in writing and art, and lack of interest in sports, made him seem eccentric to his classmates. He coped with this by giving them what they expected, adopting the persona of the Romantic Artist:

> I became affected, wore a red tie, cultivated friends outside the college, was unpatriotic, declared myself a pacifist and a Socialist, a genius. I hung reproductions of paintings by Gauguin, Van Gogh, and Paul Klee on my walls. On fine days I used to take a cushion into the quadrangle, and sitting down on it read poetry.
>
> (*WWW*, p. 33)

But then Spender met W. H. Auden, another "eccentric" under-graduate, and he eventually found himself part of the Oxford literary "gang." Auden, not quite two years older, became a mentor of sorts, giving Spender lessons in which poets were worth reading and which were a waste of time, commenting on the younger man's work and encouraging him, telling him to "drop the Shelley stunt." "The poet," Auden explained to him, was "far more like Mr. Everyman than Shelley or Keats. He cuts his hair short, wears spats, a bowler hat, and a pin-stripe city suit. He goes to the job in the bank by the suburban train" (*WWW*, p. 62). Through Auden, Spender found his way to the works of Joyce, Eliot, Woolf, and Hemingway, and began writing "poems containing references to gasworks, factories and slums" (*WWW*, p. 95). And it was in Auden's room that Spender met Christopher Isherwood for the first time.

Even before Spender met Isherwood, and even before he read anything he had written, he thought of him as "The Novelist," primarily because of Auden's respect for him. A little earlier, Isherwood had published his first novel, *All the Conspirators*, which did not get good reviews and was quietly remaindered. Yet, while for Spender "Auden seemed to us the highest peak within the range of our humble vision from the Oxford valleys, for Auden there was another peak, namely Isherwood" (*WWW*, p. 102). And for a time, Auden dangled the possibility of meeting Isherwood in front of Spender as a sort of forbidden treat. Spender had shown Auden a story he had written about his friendship with an English boy, and Auden, impressed, had shown it to Isherwood. Finally, it was Isherwood's interest in the fiction that prompted Auden to introduce the two young men.

> Our first meeting was in Auden's rooms on a bright sunny afternoon. As Auden hated the daylight, all the blinds were drawn and the electric light was on. Seated at a table covered with manuscripts were Auden and Isherwood. Auden wore a green shade over his eyes, and Isherwood looked like a schoolboy playing charades. . . . Isherwood made me a quite formal little speech saying he had read my manuscript, and that he regarded it as one of the most striking things he had read by a younger writer for a long time, and so on.
>
> (*WWW*, p. 102)

In *Lions and Shadows,* his semi-fictionalized autobiography of his "education in the twenties," Isherwood explains that he was in fact quite interested in Spender's story, which was "not quite like anything else" (p. 172) he had ever read. In that book Isherwood gives his own impressions of their first meeting:

> A few weeks later, Weston arranged a meeting with the author. He burst in upon us, blushing, sniggering loudly, contriving to trip over the edge of the carpet—an immensely tall, shambling boy of nineteen, with a great scarlet poppy-face, wild frizzy hair, and eyes the violent colour of blue-bells. His name was Stephen Savage.
>
> (*LS*, p. 173)

The following summer, Spender hand-printed Auden's first book, *Poems,* along with his own first book, *Nine Experiments.* In August, Auden left for a year in Berlin, and in his absence Spender's friendship with Isherwood flourished. Replacing Auden as Spender's "mentor," on long walks through London Isherwood spoke at length of his own life and his views on art; this began to clarify for Spender a number of his own misgivings about the quality of his personal relationships, his writing, and university life. Soon Spender became convinced that like Isherwood, who had left Cambridge without his degree, he too must eschew the university if he wanted to get beyond the superficialities of life and become a writer. Isherwood spoke to him of Germany "as the country where all the obstructions and complexities of this life were cut through" (*WWW*, p. 104), and both young men longed to go there to live and work. It was Isherwood, four years Spender's senior, who was able to first make the break with London, visiting Auden for about a week in March of 1929, then returning to Berlin more or less permanently in November. Spender himself went on holiday to Germany in the summer of 1929, and again the following year; his break with the university would not be complete, however, until early 1931.

LETTER 1

[January 1929]
University Coll[ege, Oxford]

Dear Christopher,
Here are 3 poems.[1]* I have to work now, and I found at the end of last vac. that I owed £17, so for the moment I have to make cash out of selling books from reviewing, so I have put the novel aside for the time.[2] I hope you are doing well. I am excited to know how your writing's getting on.

Will you show them to Wystan, if they are good, & when you see him? I'm not sure of his address.

Is Wystan still annoyed by Wyndham Lewis?[3]

The Enemy appears next week.[4] I don't know whether he's taken out that poem, but I asked him to.

Love, Stephen

LETTER 2

August 17 [1929]
Hotel Minerva
Bad. Hamburg

Dear Christopher,
Charles is quite dead,[5] and I have never imagined it was possible to be so happy as I have been. Now I am alone with my grandmother, & I keep wanting to speak to people & write to them. Your turn has come. Do send me a card quickly & say what you think of that. And how is Wystan? What happened at Harz?[6]

I am in love and going away with a German friend on the Rhine from Sept. 1st-9th. I stay here for a week or 10 days. On the 16th I hope Wystan will come & stay with me, but he has become silent as the tomb again. If you write, tell him I'm going away now & expect him then. But don't bother. I was sort of a prostitute to my host in Hamburg. That is an exaggeration.

Love, Stephen

Do let me hear from you *at once.* I am very lonely just now. I do so want to see you. Will you be in town Sept. 16th-Oct. 9th? Don't

---

*Notes to Part One begin on p. 39.

bother Wystan. I shall have to write him anyway. I am writing another story, & read about 40 pp. a day & take notes on it. Also, I learn German. I must know something.

I'm sorry this is all rather confused.

LETTER 3

August 25, 1929[7]
Hamburg

Dear Christopher,

I was glad to hear from you. I return to London on Sept. 9th & I've asked Wystan to come then, so I hope we shall all meet. I think your poem is awfully good, but you know I'm not a very good critic, being much too sympathetic to be impartial. I'm pleased that you liked the poem about the Port, written for Herbert List.[8] I am writhing now at the prospect of a new poem to come something like this:

> On figures met in trains with their pale faces
> Touched intimately, & yet far off, something painted on canvas,
> I brood with brow troubled like Europe
> Where they have trenched & furrowed the map.[9]

It may begin like that: I've been years thinking about it, starting long before I came out here, and now my idea is almost complete.

I am excessively happy.

I am sorry that you should be in debt. Would you like me to give you some money? I think I might have about £3. I got some money for an article to the *Spectator* the other day, & I am writing an article on the sonnets.[10]

A woman who was put in an asylum has done a portrait of me, & I have three of her pictures. She has genius, but not greatness.[11] Will show you them.

Herbert [List] & I go to the Rhine very shortly together.

Love, Stephen

Philip Snowden[12] is incredibly beautiful I think.

LETTER 4 _____

[spring, 1930]
University College, Oxford[13]

Dear Christopher,

You certainly must have been judging me very much according to "early Charles" if you thought I would be offended about the novel. Even if Cape accepts it now, I will ask them if I may withdraw it for a year.[14]

It is rather humiliating not being an infant prodigy, but still the only times I feel independent and rather grand are when I am humiliated.

I shall write my prep school story in Germany, and I will think of "Escaped" as work to be done directly I go down from here. I wish my poetry were better, I wish myself were maturer, so that I could fix the ideas instead of being overwhelmed by them when they come to me.

I bathed this morning, and yesterday I bled about a pint.[15] I was very upset and furious at the Poetry Society. It was an odd and very happy weekend spent with you and Marston. Talking to each of you in turn, and talking freely with him for the first time was like living in two different worlds, and when I saw you off, and when on Monday his life resumed its normal rowing aspect, shut off from me as if by a valve, I was slightly dazed. So I was very angry and disillusioned when I returned to all the little aesthetes.

Yesterday was one of the best days we've had for a long time. I tried to write in the morning but not very successfully. Like a fool I showed what I'd written to Dick Crossman. At least not really like a fool, because he was superb. The poem was perfectly simple, obvious, and very bad. But he said: "My dear Stephen, I don't understand your work nowadays at all." It was a grand school-masterly confession, like God saying with slight sarcasm, "I'm afraid you're much too clever for me" to someone.

I wish to heaven there was some way of getting out of this place, so that I could have a calmer life, and work at my writing. Honestly I think I have enough ideas at the moment for things I want to write to keep me occupied for six months. Damn Oxford. When can one escape from such a place and live in peace?

Thanks awfully for your company last week-end, and also for your kind letter.

Yours, Stephen

LETTER 5

[spring, 1930]
University College, Oxford[16]

Dear Christopher,

Thanks for your letter. Cape[17] wrote saying that "it was not strong enough to fight its way through," that he wanted very much to see anything else I might write as he had great confidence in my literary future, and advising me to put "Escaped" aside for a year or two.

I see now that my moral about Charles was all wrong. Charles must be very much cherished. The other day Marston asked me to stay with his family next vac., and everyone here is very gentle.

They are constructing a wooden tent in the quad. for Commem, and seeing a lot of junk under tarpaulin on the grass, I decided to sleep out last night. Instead of throwing things at me as they would have done formerly, two hearties came and slept out as well. It was really very beautiful, the skeleton of the tent, its masts and stays, like a ship, and in the morning the swallows dipping in the shade and sunlight.

Here is a poem I hope you will like.[18]

Saying 'good morning' becomes painful
And talking at meals, since words
Fall cumbrously about our feet like swords.
Hours we've braved out together through a lull
And then mouth to mouth we've fared the storm:
Speaking across tables, a form of possession
Like taking your wrists & feeling your lips warm.

But chance 'good mornings,' seeing you in the street,
Talking at the door, or when each other starts
Looks eye to eye & then breaks away,
Is more than I can stand. We should not meet
So lightly. Let us break our hearts
Not casually, but on a stated day.

Love, Stephen

LETTER 6 ——————————————————————————————————
Thursday [fall, 1930]
[Oxford]

Dear Christopher,
Yesterday at lunch I saw [Marston] and he told me of his decision.[19] He said that he would like to go on seeing me in an ordinary hearty way, but he refused to recognise anything further beyond that, or really even discuss it. He said he thought he was probably being a cad, and that he was very sorry. I said that if it was to be like that, the advances must come this term from his side; that now I wouldn't try and arrange meetings for him and bother him about going out; and that if he did meet me, the greatest injustice he could do me was to meet me out of pity, that he must do it because he wanted to. He owned that in that case he probably wouldn't see me.

I talked a lot more about his own life and so on and left quite cordially. But this evening I rushed by him in the lodge because I couldn't stand seeing him.

The worst thing he said yesterday was that he had great difficulty in meeting me because he felt uncomfortable with me. I can't stand seeing him and I'm not dining in hall tonight, and now I feel that I won't ever dine in hall this term.

Christopher, this is an utter failure, and what's to be done? I suppose I'll feel cheerfuller tomorrow, and finally I suppose that I'll forget him, even though I meet him in the streets, and am always reminded. But still I've failed, and the failure is much more my fault than his that he should be "uncomfortable" with me.

All the same I feel quite hungry and I'll go and eat somewhere now. It's done me good to write this down.
Love, Stephen

LETTER 7 ——————————————————————————————————
[fall, 1930]
University College, Oxford[20]

Dear Christopher,
I haven't heard from you in months. Like everyone else in paradise you forget about us here below and never write letters.

I have no poem or anything good enough to send you. There is a nice story about hay making, but I haven't a copy of that at present. I may send it later. But don't wait for it to write. I am working hard at my Schools & at reading to see whether anything will come out of it. I am still living in hopes of finding a mistress here. I am going to have another shot tonight. I am learning German, for June in Hamburg, then Berlin. I heard Dick Crossman read a paper on art last night. It is a good and wonderful life full of numerous events. After all I will send you a rotten poem.[21] Oh, I have stopped being in love with Marston; but I still catch my breath when he comes into the room.

It is raining. Sunday. And very Oxford, like rain falling on tombstones. I feel rather as if I had tossed myself off fifty times in the last hour. But I haven't because of tonight.

I think that's all about me, so now, as Dame Henrietta Barnett[22] says, let us pass to more interesting subjects, though not to our wonderful garden suburbs. Christopher, this is written as though I were about four. I'm so sorry, but that's what this place makes me feel like.

I am coming out to Berlin in September in order to see a girl whom I hope perhaps to marry. Don't for God's sake tell her that, if you see her. Will you write to her & say that you're a friend of mine & I've written and may you see her, etc.? I think you will like her. She is Russian, or rather Lithuanian. She is exciting and very nice. Very young, only 17. Very funny indeed. Jewish.

Her name is:

Fraulein Gisa Soloweitschik
Berlin-Wilm
Konstrauzerstr. 10.

Her telephone no. *Oliva 2004*

She speaks English. Her brother Wladimir is a film-director or something in Ufa. He also composes jazz-music. I think you will be interested. There seems nothing else to say. I hope to hear from you. What are you writing? What are you doing? When are you coming home?

Love, Stephen

LETTER 8

[winter, 1930]
63, St. John's, Oxford[23]

Dear Christopher,

Thanks very much for your letter. Yes do go & see Gisa. I enclose now this story which I will re-write in June.[24] So I do not send it feeling satisfied with it, but hoping that you may help me.

Life here is more pleasant, because recently it has again become pure farce. I have discovered a great passage in Gide which is rather like my life with my friends: "ses amis, pendant leur sommeil ou du moins pendant le sommeil de Bernard, s'étaient rapprochés—"[25] I spent some weeks trying to seduce someone this term, and at last one evening feeling that the time had come I began a moral discussion. But this one before I had properly got going interrupted me: "You know, Stephen, since I met you my life's entirely altered. When I first knew you I used to masturbate and I used to read pornographic books. But now, after being with you, all that's stopped. I don't masturbate and I'm absolutely pure!"

So I must forsake the well of loneliness I suppose & take up the challenge and start a religious movement. "Vous aimez le petit musicien." "Oh comme le sable était beau! . . ."

All this time I am writing. Have to write 16 pp. foolscap a week for tutors.

Last week-end Wystan came down bringing a friend called Johnny Walker. Pale. Red lips. Black hair. Small nose. Dark eyes. Pathetically dressed in a double breasted suit made of some coarse stuff, proud but ill-fitting: a scarf round his throat made of bright blue artificial silk. I think he was a friend of Layard's & that W was trying to get him a job and thought that a day at Oxford might amuse him. We went to a cinema in the afternoon, then the boy went home & Wystan went out with me that evening. The next day W sent me a p.c. "I hear you held Johnny's hand yesterday in the Super. Stephen, is this manners?" I felt rather annoyed, because I can't make out whether he was trying to be funny or really angry or what. Anyhow it was not true and quite funny.[26]

I am writing two more stories now. This letter is rather silly, I think, but anything written at Oxford needs an apology.

Important. Will you send the story on to Gisa Soloweitschik,

Berlin-Wilm, Konstauzerstr, 10, when you have done with it?
Now I must write my essay.

Yours, Stephen

LETTER 9

January 2 [1931]
10, Frognal,
Hampstead, N.W.3[27]

Dear Christopher,

I have just read your novel[28] again, and have now taken it to the typist. I was very moved by it. I cannot say more. I cannot judge the last part, because my sense of balance in its relation to the whole was spoiled by the fact that I have read the first 2½ parts three or four times.

I am depressed beyond words just now. I don't know why, but I have a feeling of melancholia which quite surprises me. I takes me like a disease, and I watch its symptoms, as though it were something inside myself. I feel drawn to you now, and profoundly touched by your book, because you will know what I feel. It is funny how well you have done the relationship between Edward and Margaret, which is very like the relationship with my stepmother. Just before I read the passage in your book, having written two final letters to her, I had been so convinced of my injustice, that I had taken refuge in an "exaggerated apology." But the nausea I feel now goes much further than my relationship with my stepmother.

However, it is carefully timed. I shall go out with friends to the theatre this evening and will be well. Then on February 1st I shall join you in Germany. How nice that will be! But how many years will it take before I can emerge from the waters at the point where you have emerged? It is though I had to *swim* that rotten Channel. I have always been trying to build tunnels under it; now I shall give up. I see it has got to be swum.

I loved your book. I look forward most intensely to seeing you. Please give my love to Walter.[29]

With Best Love from Stephen

Notes to Part One

[1] The editor was not provided with copies of these manuscripts. According to a note from Christopher Isherwood, "the poems are 'Never being but always at the edge of being,' 'Holiday over the sea,' 'The Port' (the latter two are on different paper)." "Never being" and "The Port" appeared in *Twenty Poems* (Oxford: Basil Blackwood, 1930).

[2] According to a note on the manuscript, Spender completed his first novel, *The Temple*, in November of 1929.

[3] Wyndham Lewis, English novelist, essayist, and artist, published his *The Philosophy of the Melting Pot* in 1929; this is perhaps a reference to that book.

[4] Wyndham Lewis' magazine, *The Enemy*, lasted for three issues, between 1927 and 1929.

[5] "Charles" was a character in an early unpublished story written by Spender.

[6] According to *CaHK*, in July Isherwood had visited Auden at the village of Rotheheutte in the Harz Mountains. Auden "welcomed Christopher as one welcomes a guest to one's household; he had the air of owning the village and the villagers" (p. 8). Because of trouble with the police, however, the pair soon left for Amsterdam.

[7] Postmark (postcard). Return address reads, "Next address: S. Spender, 10 Frognal, Hampstead, N.W.3."

[8] "The Port" (see note 1, this section).

[9] If this poem was ever completed, it is unpublished.

[10] Spender's first published article, "Problems of the Poet and Public," appeared in the *Spectator*, 143 (August 3, 1929), pp. 152-53. The "article on the sonnets," if finished, remained unpublished.

[11] Unidentified.

[12] Viscount Snowden, an authority on national finance, served as Chancellor of the Exchequer in 1924, and again from 1929 to 1931.

[13] Written on University College stationery.

[14] *The Temple* (see Letter 1). "Escaped" was an early title.

[15] "Savage's nose-bleeding (now long since cured) was famous, at this period: Weston called him 'the fountain.' Without the least warning, at all times of the day, the blood would suddenly squirt from his

39

nostrils, as if impelled by the appalling mental pressure within that scarlet, accusing face . . ." (*LS*, p. 225).

[16] Written on University College stationery.

[17] Jonathan Cape would publish Spender's first prose book, *The Destructive Element*, in 1935. He had published Isherwood's first novel in 1928.

[18] Published as "Saying 'Good Morning' becomes Painful" (number ten of the "Marston Poems") in *Twenty Poems*. Not reprinted.

[19] In *WWW*, Spender explains that after a certain period of time in his friendship with "Marston," he found it necessary to write him a letter explaining his strong feelings for him. "He wrote back saying that we should meet. When we met he explained that he in no way responded to my emotion. . . . I insisted that we should not meet again. However, as we were of the same college, not to do so proved impossible. So now we used to meet at intervals, usually in teashops in Oxford or London, and talk seriously, with a kind of sadness" (p. 66).

[20] Written on University College stationery.

[21] The manuscript has been lost.

[22] Dame Henrietta Barnett (1851-1936) was the founder of the Henrietta Barnett School in 1912. Her publications included *Making of the Home*, *How to Mind the Baby*, and *Worship and Work*.

[23] Written on Oxford University English Club stationery.

[24] The story has been lost.

[25] "His friends, during their sleep, or at least during the sleep of Bernard, came closer together." (André Gide, *The Counterfeiters*). And later, "You like the little musician." "Oh how beautiful the sand was . . ." (Gide, *If It Die*).

[26] John Layard, an anthropologist, was the model for Barnard in Isherwood's *LS;* he introduced Auden to the work of the American psychologist Homer Lane. Johnny Walker is unidentified.

[27] Written on Spender's personal stationery with address imprinted.

[28] *The Memorial.* Two months later Jonathan Cape, the publisher of Isherwood's first novel, rejected the manuscript. Spender carried it to John Lehmann, and on September 2 the novel was accepted for publication by the Hogarth Press.

[29] Isherwood's character Otto Nowak (in *Goodbye to Berlin*) was modeled on Walter.

PART TWO

1932–1935

Stephen Spender left Oxford without his degree in early 1931. During the summer of 1928, he had hand-set and printed Auden's *Poems* in a small edition himself, and a few months after leaving Oxford he had been instrumental in bringing about the acceptance of Christopher Isherwood's *The Memorial* by the Hogarth Press. His own work had appeared in 1931 in Michael Roberts' influential *New Signatures*, and he was publishing both poetry and reviews in the magazines. The following year, *Oxford Poetry* was dedicated to Spender (along with Auden and Day Lewis), and by the winter of 1932, Faber and Faber had accepted his first major book of poetry, *Poems*.

Spender was already beginning to divide his time about equally between England and the Continent, a habit that would persist throughout the decade. Earlier he had taken rather idyllic summer holidays in Hamburg, and then lived for a while near Isherwood in a Berlin which was plagued by increasing inflation, unemployment, and poverty, and political struggles among myriad factions; there he gradually became aware that their lives and "the carefree personal lives of our friends were façades in front of the immense social chaos" (*WWW*, p. 131) which was approaching. In November of 1932, he took the first of many trips to Spain, looking for a place to settle perhaps permanently with a German friend named Hellmut. Two months later, however, the sojourn (described in detail in the first few letters of this section) ended disastrously, although it did provide him with material for his short story "The Dead Islands." By the end of January, Spender had returned to London alone, and for a time he was caught up in "a literary-social life of luncheons, teas, and week-ends at country houses" (*WWW*, p. 142).

Poems was published in January, 1933. It was an accomplished first volume and fairly well received. Spender had retained some undergraduate love poems from his earlier privately printed volumes (much of the "Marston" sequence, for example), and these stood alongside poems of political commitment. In its blurb, Faber announced that "technically, these poems appear to make a definite step forward in English poetry," yet, as Samuel Hynes points out, the reviewers fixed not on technique but on Spender's social and political engagement: "Mr. Spender is conscious of his social heritage of chaos and despair," wrote Herbert Read in the *Adelphi*. "Perhaps the book's most notable quality is its social consciousness, and the perfect

fusion of this often too intractable material with the poetic idiom."
The *Times Literary Supplement* followed suit, its reviewer commenting that Spender should be commended for his "love and pity
towards the hungry, the unemployed, and the oppressed."[1]* The
book sold well enough to be reprinted the following year.

Originally, Spender had intended to dedicate *Poems* to Isherwood;
the novelist was, after all, one of his closest friends and a major
influence on his work.[2] During the winter of 1932, however, just
before Spender left for Spain, the two had a brief falling-out. In *WWW*,
Spender lays the blame for the quarrel on himself:

> Christopher came to London at the same time as myself. He met
> most of my friends, shortly before or after I had met them. He found
> that I had already told them most of his stories, and that I had been
> indiscreet. Moreover, he disliked seeing me transformed from his
> Berlin Disciple into a London literary figure.
>
> (*WWW*, p. 174)

Isherwood's version of the cause of the episode differs slightly. While
he agrees that he was probably annoyed at Spender's indiscretions, he
had something else on his mind; while the two were living in Berlin,
Spender had begun to "get on his nerves":

> Christopher's deeper motive in quarreling with Stephen was to get
> him out of Berlin altogether. I don't think he consciously knew this
> at the time. It is obvious to me now. Christopher regarded Berlin as
> his territory. He was actually becoming afraid that Stephen would
> scoop him by writing Berlin stories of his own and rushing them into
> print!
>
> (*CaHK*, p. 107)

After a particularly difficult meeting at a party at the home of William
Plomer, Isherwood wrote Spender a letter informing him that if he
returned to Berlin, he himself would not. The result of this was,
according to Spender, two-fold: first, he decided against returning to
Berlin; second, it made him break his "habit of dependence on Christopher" (*WWW*, p. 174). The two reconciled soon after, before Spender went to Spain and Isherwood returned to Berlin, but for a while, it
was an uneasy truce. And when *Poems* appeared, it carried no dedication whatsoever.[3]

---

*Notes to Part Two begin on p. 83.

Soon after his return to London from Spain, Spender, reeling over the difficulties of the previous few months, was lonely and depressed. He thought of advertisting for a companion in the newspapers, but then by chance he met a young man and decided to hire him as his secretary. Tony (he is called Jimmy Younger in both *WWW* and *CaHK*) came from a background alien to Spender's experience. His family was working-class, and not only had he not been to the university, but he had run away from home to join the army. He was just out of the service and was one of the thirties' unemployed when the two men met, and as their relationship grew beyond the bounds of employer-employee, it was perhaps this different background, Spender admits, which drew him to Tony:

> The differences of class and interest between Jimmy and me certainly did provide some element of mystery which corresponded almost to a difference in sex. I was in love, as it were, with his background, his soldiering, his working-class home. Nothing moved me more than to hear him tell stories of the Cardiff streets of Tiger Bay. . . . When Jimmy talked of such things, I was perhaps nearer poetry than talking to most of my fellow poets.
>
> (*WWW*, p. 184)

As with Isherwood, Spender's friendship with Tony was sometimes volatile and always intense; they would remain companions until late 1936, when Spender married Inez Pearn and Tony left to fight in the war in Spain.

In the spring of 1933, Spender and Tony travelled to Italy, and the following year they went to Vienna and Mlini, a small town on the coast of Yugoslavia. During this time, Spender had accepted a contract from Cape to write a book on Henry James, but he wasn't having much success finishing it; nor was he writing many poems. While he and Tony enjoyed one another's company, they argued often (usually over trivial things), and Spender was beginning to realize that if he "were to live with anyone it could not be a man" (*WWW*, p. 185). While staying in Mlini, they met a divorced American woman named Muriel Gardiner (Elizabeth in *WWW*) who was vacationing there with her child. She was a student of medicine and psychology in Vienna, and after a few days, Spender began to be quite taken with her, watching her activities as if through "a curtain of wonder, which

I knew at some time I would draw aside" (*WWW*, p. 193). Not long after she had returned to her studies in Vienna, Tony developed trouble with his appendix. A physician recommended an operation, so the two men travelled to Muriel's apartment where they stayed while she arranged for a surgeon and a hospital. It was during the period of Tony's convalescence that Spender and Muriel lived together in her house in Wiener Wald, a few miles from Vienna, and were for a time lovers.

On January 30, 1933, Adolf Hitler had been appointed Chancellor of Germany, and, a year later, in February, the anti-fascist Austrian Social Democrats were defeated by government forces in Vienna. Soon after Muriel and Spender met, she joined a group of Austrian Socialists and put her money and her apartment at their disposal; for his part, Spender set aside his study of James and began *Vienna*, his long poem about the defeat of the Social Democrats. In his essay "Poetry and Revolution" (published in Michael Roberts' second anthology, *New Country*, in March, 1933), Spender had argued that while the artist must reflect a social consciousness, his primary function was to tell the truth; he must at all times be cautious of being "led astray into practical politics." *Vienna* is assuredly a political poem—it contains a sympathetic account of the struggle of the Left during the February Uprising—yet it is more, a young man's troubled search for his own identity in the chaos and ruins of war:

> In part this expressed my indignation at the suppression of the Viennese Socialists by Dollfuss, Fey and Starhemberg; but in part it was concerned with a love relationship. I meant to show that the two experiences were different, yet related. For both were intense, emotional and personal, although one was public, the other private.
>
> (*WWW*, p. 192)

It was written in just a few months, and published by Faber and Faber in November, 1934,[4] dedicated to Muriel.

By 1935, Christopher Isherwood, who had moved to a flat in Copenhagen from Berlin, had completed work on a film script, *Little Friend*, and had finished his novel *The Lost*, published that year by the Hogarth Press under the title *Mr. Norris Changes Trains*. In January he and Auden had finished collaborating on their first play, *Where is Francis?*, staged later that year by Rupert Doone's Group Theatre as *The Dog Beneath the Skin*. Isherwood's primary personal concern at this time, reflected in the correspondence, was the welfare of his German friend and companion Heinz. Heinz was a German citizen and the threat of compulsory military service had been building in Germany for some time. On March 16, Hitler instituted conscription, denouncing the Treaty of Versailles, and for the next several months Isherwood was involved in numerous costly and complex legal intrigues in an attempt to keep Heinz out of the army.

During the writing of *Vienna* and after, Spender was dividing his time between England and Austria. He had returned to work on his study of James, which by now had evolved into a major project. Originally, the book had been intended as a rather straight-forward narrative of the novelist's early years, but by the time it was finished it had become a study of modern literature and politics. Part One of the book dealt with James, Part Two with Yeats, Eliot, and Lawrence, and Part Three with a number of younger writers; these were all figures, Spender explained, who were "political-moral artists who were in the dilemma of Hamlet: they found their lives fixed in a world in which there were no external symbols for their inner sense of values. There was no power, and no glory."[5] Published in March of 1935, *The Destructive Element: A Study of Modern Writers and Beliefs* was dedicated to Rosamond Lehmann and Wogan Philipps, and according to its dust-jacket blurb, it was "the first critical work of a young writer whose poetry has already made him a representative figure of the youngest generation."

While finishing *The Destructive Element*, Spender had begun making notes for the revision of his unpublished novel *The Temple*, and now he was writing poetry, reviews, and articles, and working on the stories which would be collected in *The Burning Cactus* the following year. Also, he was attempting to turn *Vienna* into a play, and he planned to translate a selection of Hölderlin's poems for Heinemann with Edwin Muir. In the early summer, he left London with Tony for visits to Vienna, Mlini, and Innsbruck, seeing Muriel briefly. In August, Spender and Isherwood spent a few days together in Amsterdam, where Spender unexpectedly arrived for Isherwood's birthday party given by Gerald Hamilton; soon after, the two made plans for a winter vacation in Sintra with Tony and Heinz. On December 10, Spender, Isherwood, Tony, and Heinz left Antwerp for Portugal, where they remained until mid-March of 1936.

LETTER 10

> December 4 [1932]
> as from: c/o Thos Cook
> Placa Cataluña, Barcelona
> [Malaga]

Dear Christopher,

Thank you very much for your letter which I should have answered some time ago, but we have been very unsettled during the last three weeks. We have quite failed to find a house here or in the neighborhood which is either at a reasonable price or furnished. The only possibility was a house in a fishing village near here but that was unfurnished and in any case we hated the village. We can't very well go on living in this hotel because each day we spend far too much money, and also Hellmut has nothing to do. So tomorrow we are going back to Barcelona where we know that we can get rooms with a kitchen, which he can run. It is all slightly disappointing, but returning to Barcelona has consolations because there are cinemas, concerts, books, and a certain amount of social life for Hellmut, with the German Theatre which he wants to act in. As long as I can get a room where I can work, I shall be very happy. This tour has served a very good purpose because we have been away quite alone together & got to like each other more, but I am sorry about the house & it had never occurred to either of us that it was impossible to get such a thing. "The South" is rather a snag because in December it suddenly gets very cold here the moment the sun goes in, and during the last three days it has rained & blown from the East. There is no heating at all in the hotels anywhere, so the result is that the people who are sent here for cures die off like flies. I expect that is really why they are sent here. But it is rather unfortunate if one gets amongst them by mistake: I am unscathed at present but Hellmut has a very bad feverish cold.

We have done quite a lot in the last few days. We came here in a cargo boat which made us very ill in the end. Not only was the weather storming but all the food was cooked in camp oil, so I was very very sick indeed. We have got to return by one of these boats, but we are going to take our own food, in case we should need any, but I do not think that is very likely, as an extremely shrill East wind is blowing and tonight the sky is a transparent pale apple green colour scrawled upon angrily with a few pitch-black charcoaled clouds. In the course of our house-hunting we decided that we should give up the use of agents and walk ourselves to Gibraltar, as Hellmut was unwell. Food is an awful problem here, because having an ulcer of the stomach makes eating things cooked in oil absolutely disastrous, so directly we get anywhere out of the way Hellmut has to starve or live on bread. Anyhow Gibraltar was a very comic place full of English policemen & sailors & soldiers & naval & military police & demure little officers' wives and shops all stuffed with books for little English girls & boys called the *Kind Shepherd, The Book of Saints & Heroes,* etc., as an antidote, I suppose, to the spicing of something Eastern & vicious which sneaks along the gutters of Gibraltar & glares through an occasional lighted window, like a memory of the more "outpost-ish" satires of the British Empire Exhibition. We were only allowed to stay in Gibraltar for one day, on account of our obviously suspicious appearance. Hellmut loved Gibraltar & we spent the evening looking at sailors dancing with each other: but not very much of the evening, because at 11 o'clock exactly a lot of whistles were blown & the police ordered everyone to bed. We then went to Algeciras. Algeciras is a little port in the shadow of Gibraltar as it were. You can see Africa quite a short way across the Straits of Gibraltar & I kept on thinking of that poem of Browning's in which he thinks of about 12 rhymes to the syllable "ay" and then breaks down badly in the last line with "Africa."[6] Is one meant to say "Africay" or is the sudden change to "a" very effective? I have never dared to ask anyone before, so please do not mention that I ask this now. In the hotel in Algeciras there were two Americans, mother & son with a dog. They felt the cold so badly that they used, with absolute frankness, to come down to meals in their greatcoats. They, like us, were would-be dwellers in Gibraltar, but they had not been allowed to stay there on account of the dog, which the English suspected of espionage. They were returning to America in a few days from Gibraltar but when they went through "Gib," as the best people call it, they had to be accompanied by a policeman in order that he might see what the dog was up to all the time. Having failed to find a house in Algeciras we returned here, in order to make more inquiries.

We live in a very domestic way which I like extremely. We have bought a cooker & we make our own supper & breakfast always. Hellmut is very homely & very good at managing things. It really will be awfully nice when we have a place of our own; far nicer than living amidst scenery which staggers the beholder with its obvious genius and which one follows breathlessly, wondering how long it can keep it up, just as if one were Gerald Gould reading his batch of novels in the *Observer*.[7] The inhabitants of this coast are mostly pimps, idiots, & cripples, whatever anyone may say to the contrary. The children are particularly nasty. If they see you are a foreigner they run after you shouting "penny" "penny" in a mechanical, harsh, joyless way which would cure any lover of children. The people spit everywhere. In hotels, restaurants, in circles all around one's feet. One feels so incorrigibly a foreigner here that it is really very unpleasant. One would never be at home or accepted here, one feels: one's presence is rather inexcusable. Malaga is full of pimps who come up to us and say "Good evening. Do you want your girl?" with the discreet air of guides about to show one round a cathedral. All this is rather irritating to both of us, especially to Hellmut who gets very angry with the children. On our walk we went to one village where we were practically stoned by crowds of syphilitic, joyless, old-looking children. It was sinister.

I have not been able to do much work except to keep a journal, which I have done assiduously.

It is of course all right about Georg,[8] though it is rather saddening to hear he is like that. If you see him again, I suppose you couldn't put in a word of good influence could you? Because I am sure his father has work for him at home.

There is no more news. Write again soon & please excuse this very hurried letter.

Love, Stephen

Hellmut thanks you for the greetings & greets you. Please greet Heinz from us. Also greet William R[obson] -S[cott].[9] I haven't read Hemingway.[10] I haven't got Karl H's[11] negatives; I expect they are now being lost in the moving at home. If I remember it, enclosed is a picture of Hellmut. If you see Wolfgang Harman, *please* get my copy of *The Memorial* out of him. Most important.

If you care to read Lawrence's *Last Poems*,[12] I sent my copy to Roger Sessions, bei Andreae, 126, Kurfurstenstrasse.[13]

LETTER 11

January 5 [1933]
Barcelona

Dear Christopher,

Thank you very much for your letter which I read twice & then accidentally dropped in the street. I was very sad at having lost it & I came back hours later & hunted about for it, in vain.

Have you ever read this from H. James: "But I come back, I come back, as I say, I all throbbingly and yearningly & passionately, oh mon bon, come back to this way that is clearly the only one in which I can do anything now, and that will open out to me more and more, and that has overwhelming reasons pleading all beautifully in its breast. What really happens is that the closer I get to the problem of the application of it in any particular case the more I get *into* that application, so that the more doubts & torments fall away from me, the more I know where I am, the more everything spreads & shines & draws me on & I'm justified of my logic & my passion. . . . Oh celestial, soothing, sanctifying process, with all the high sane forces of the sacred time fighting, through it, on my side! Let me fumble it gently and patiently out—with fever & fidget laid to rest—as in the old enchanted months! It only looms, it only shines and shimmers, *too* beautiful and too interesting; it only hangs there too rich & too full & with too much to give and to pay; it only presents itself too admirable & too vividly, too straight and square & vivid, as a little organic and effective Action. . . ."[14]

[My life with Hellmut] is being a failure. Two days have passed since I wrote that sentence and now it has been a failure and it is at an end as Hellmut has gone back to Basel.

Dr. Möring has played an incredibly bad joke on me by sending his friend Kirk here. He wrote some time ago saying that the dear boy was much better & could we find him a room when he was on his way to Minorca, for a short time. I consulted with Hellmut who was quite keen on his coming, so I wrote politely saying that we would find room if he ever needed it & then forgot all about it. Then suddenly I had a letter announcing that Kirk was coming almost at once, and a day or two later he appeared. Humphrey [Spender] was also here when he came as he has been here the last fortnight or so and is going to stay on now for another day or two—Hellmut is a homosexual of the "major unknown authors of our time" type, so that the arrival of Kirk led to all sorts of absurd dramas being performed which ended by breaking up our life, which was perhaps not a bad thing. But the bad thing is that two evenings ago K had arranged to meet us at a restaurant & he turned up half an hour late loaded with presents for all of us. It was quite ten minutes before I realized that something was wrong. He was drunk in a very serious macabre kind of way, and apart from his speech which was very odd & rather frightening, the most notable thing about his appearance was that his eyes were fixed and did not seem to move at all. He left us after supper & refused to go anywhere with us. We arranged to meet at 11 the next morning but instead of his turning up, a very sumptuous present of chocolates for Hellmut arrived plus *Pan* by Hamsun, [15] the first four pp. of which were inscribed with a very long dedication from Kirk which was quite illegible. I called on him at 12 and he was out; I went back at 6 and he was lying on his bed, but would not open the door of his room. I went back once again & got into his room and tried to talk to him but he talked absolute nonsense, not as if he were drunk, but as if he were in a dream. This morning Humphrey & I went for a walk & we saw Kirk in the distance in front of us making water in front of a telegraph post, so he has been like this for 48 hours now. In the restaurant he also gave Humphrey a love letter 8 pages long, so Humphrey is extremely alarmed. I am also furious because H is now going away & I will be quite alone with Kirk. As a matter of fact I have quite decided that if things get bad I shall simply report the matter to the American consulate & then go home, because this atmosphere of insanity is intolerable. It is really ridiculous of Möring not to have said a word about Kirk's state, not to have said what we should do if this sort of thing occurred. I wrote to him yesterday saying that I would accept absolutely no responsibility for Kirk, and that if I felt I could not stand this any longer I would return to London in the same day, as I do not want to be here with two lunatics any more than one. The final blow is that Kirk in order to be removed will have to be lent money & I have got so bad that my only reserve is half of Hellmut's savings, which he very kindly left me in case I should have to go back, so I really don't see how I can lend Kirk this money. Kirk is of an old family in a Southern State & the whole atmosphere of him is very Faulkner, but I have never wanted to live in a book by Faulkner.

Did you get the photo I sent at Christmas?

Humphrey sends greetings.

I think I shall stay here till Jan. 31st, as it is so cheap. But if I go

before then I shall send you a card.
Greetings to Heinz & W[ystan].
Love, Stephen

LETTER 12

January 10 [1933]
as from 43, Boundary Road
London N.W.8.
[Barcelona]

Dear Christopher,
I send you my book [*Poems*]. It looks very nice but the blurb seems to have been written out of pure malice,[16] and I am afraid it will annoy Wystan. I did not see it until yesterday when they sent the copies of the book. I wrote to Faber today, criticizing the blurb.

I am going away from here on Thursday—before then I hope that Möring will do something about Kirk. Running a place like this just for oneself is very depressing. Also I never have a moment's peace now because people keep on coming in to show me & the house to prospective occupants. Lastly Kirk has now been solidly drunk for exactly a week, so he is not a very good companion. He is so mad about drink that one night when he had none he stole a saucepan of mustard from the landlady's kitchen & ate all of that. I gave him some money to send a telegram to Möring, but he got drunk with it instead. He drank ¾ of a litre of alcohol for lighting stoves with this morning. That was taken away from him so he started drinking his hair oil. It is really very nasty, and he is utterly weak & behaves, eats, slobbers, whimpers, etc, like an animal. I wrote to Möring & I got Hellmut to telephone him today that he should come at once. But the Spanish post only dribbles letters of days ago out with such replies as: "Let's go to Mallorca and write lovely books or have long walks along the dreaming salt smelling tenderly tickled shores—according to our gifts." Today I had another letter of the same sort. But I suppose he must get the telegram. I also have made an arrangement with a German at Kirk's house that if anything bad happens they should go to the American consulate. The people at the house where he is are extremely nice & have offered to nurse him. The German is delighted because he has hypnotic powers which he exercises over Kirk in order to get him to sleep. This is where the Southern States style of Faulkner merges into the Southern States + Paris style of Julian Green, *Le Voyageur sur La Terre,* & once more shows that life is larger than art. [17]

You will surmise that the Spanish episode has been rather a fiasco, but I can give you no idea how instructive it has been. Hellmut & Kirk were almost text books of certain types of neurotic behavior. In fact the worst of neurosis is that people who are neurotic tend to become examples of their particular type of neurosis & they lack human interest. For instance when Hellmut went away although I felt very lonely for a day or two, it was impossible to miss him because he was quite lacking in the traits of a personality which one misses in people. Whereas I still miss Georg although he never shared my life to 1/10th of the same extent as Hellmut: but he did certain things which were unforgetably Georg's. For instance I remember him sitting an hour or so at my desk trying to copy my signature to see if he could forge a cheque successfully.

I am going for 3 days to Paris & then to London. Above is my London address. Please write. I expect this letter crosses one from you.

Love, Stephen

LETTER 13

January 23 [1933]
43 Boundary Road
[London] N.W.8.

Dear Christopher,

I am so sorry I did not reply to your letter but during the past few days whenever I have had spare moments I have been working. . . . Did Robson-Scott ever return my *Sado?* [18] You answered this question before in the letter which I lost in Barcelona & the answer I forget.

I want to shit but it is far too cold to go into another room: that will give you some idea how cold it is here. I can imagine what it must be like in Berlin. I left Barcelona because my life there was so penitential that finally I decided I might just as well be putting in a few months of London. The day before I left I sent Kirk to Ibiza as I had a letter from Möring explaining that he was really only being sent to the islands to die. Möring said he had not told me about the drink because Kirk entreated him not to, but I think the reason must partly have been because Möring after having spent all his money & nervous strength on three years of useless struggling with Kirk was absolutely determined to have nothing more to do with him and therefore was bound to shove him on to other people, and of course he knew that if he consulted me I would refuse to have Kirk there. This seems to me quite reasonable and I am extremely sorry for them both because it can be no pleasure to Möring to reap the curses of his friends & acquaintances. We managed to get Kirk on to the ship sober & then we left him there. I heard from his this morning so he has got to Ibiza.

My book [*Poems*] appeared on Thursday so I have had no reviews yet, but Faber wrote & said they had a lot of enquiries about it from reviewers. Also it will be well reviewed by Plomer in *The Referee*, by someone in *The Manchester Guardian*, by Herbert Read in *The Adelphi*, and by [Michael] Roberts in *The Listener*. So that & one or two smaller things will give it a start. It is selling very well already apparently in the shops in Kensington, Baker Street & Charing X Rd, and I am sure it will sell in the universities. So I have hopes of there being two editions. I will tell you later what the reviewers say. I am so glad you like it.[19] I have written 4 poems since then, but their (or my) extreme (newly acquired) modesty have prevented me showing them to anyone. I also did a bad essay for the Hogarth anthology & I sent them three of these poems. But unfortunately the entire collection was lost in the Spanish post. I have fears that they may be found.[20] One day I may show you the journal I did of our tour because perhaps it is the thing that would interest you most.

I don't know at all about plans as I am so overdrawn. I have a room here £13 extra where I am left very much to myself; in fact the room is outside the apartment & I have a view [?] of my own. From now on I am going to try & live at least six months a year in England. If my book pays off my debts I shall go abroad in May, first for 14 days to Paris then for 14 days to Berlin, and then, I think, to the Salz Kammergut. After the refinements of Hellmut, Georg now stands mountain high in my estimation. When I quarrelled with Georg it was only on principle, and I can never remember a time when I wasn't delighted to see him. He was never wearisome and although he was "crazy" about getting money he wasn't really mercenary even at the worst of times and he never grumbled about anything. I will write to him soon. If you see him you might hint to him that if he writes to me I might come back in May. But perhaps it is best not, because although I long to see him & certainly will see him, he was far too normal & his niceness lay really in the kind of irresponsibility about everything, even his own interest, which also made a relationship with him impossible. . . .

I am making things much easier for myself in London by working hard and by not seeing more than one or two people each day. If I can keep this up & then if I can find a bedfellow this life should be quite bearable till May. It is infinitely better now that we have left that huge house. Bed-sitting rooms are much nicer than several rooms because one's always in the same atmosphere, so I find I can always take up anything I am working at at anytime and go on with it.

William [Plomer] is well & is bringing out Rhodes[21] in February. I met [E. M.] Forster two days ago with [Joe] Ackerley[22] & liked him very much, though he is so shy that it makes one feel embarrassed. John [Lehmann] seems very much nicer: he has stopped being a Victorian statesman & now looks like a drawing of Rue conquering noble beauty by Aubrey Beardsley. He will soon catch up with the Boer War & Limehouse nights. (These remarks, I feel, might all, or all might have been made at one or another time myself.) I spend most of my evenings in the Amusement Park near Marble Arch or the Haymarket. London seems much improved. The other day a cissy friend of Humphrey's got off a bus, and as he alighted the conductor smirked & said, "What a short ride you've been," so Eddy said "Never mind, I'll come a longer one next time." Two days ago I went to Sadler's Wells with my sister. I did not know whether we were in the right tube for Angel, so I held out our tickets to the collector and said "Angel?" in a querying voice. "I am," he replied with an enticing smile.

Barcelona is certainly the most red hot revolutionary place I have ever been in.[23] That is to say in the last days that I was there all the police were not only armed with loaded rifles but they also trained the rifles. But as I knew nothing about Spanish politics I didn't really get very thrilled: not nearly so much as in Berlin.

I'm glad your uncle sent your allowance. I'm sorry you've had the flu.

When I have six poems I will send them.

Love to Heinz & best love to Georg if you see him.

Best love, Stephen

LETTER 14

Wednesday
[February, 1933]
43 Boundary Road
[London] N.W.8.[24]

Dear Christopher,

Thank you very much for your card. It is very grey and yellow here also and I am beginning already to feel nausea at London. I read eagerly the news about Germany and am filled with appropriate feelings of hatred plus despair.[25]

Not many reviews have appeared yet, but Clarke's was the only bad one. I have no copy but will send you when I have them. There was a long & good review in the [New] Statesman, also in The Listener, & a positively ecstatic one in The Adelphi by Herbert Read.[26]

...I see quite a lot of people now who lead the lives of luggers, persevering, scrupulous, unflagging. I realize now much more acutely than I did before, because I see myself bound to take a choice, that they are ascetic. They were brought up as Puritans and now that they are ruins one sees the face in a mirror, but it is the same face. When I was seventeen I was terrified of sex because I thought some terrible doom would be accomplished with it: now I am older I am terrified of not-sex for reasons of health, because I don't want to become dried up, because I am afraid that I shall get older and then it will be too late and "life" will have flowed away. The motives are in each case priestly impulses. So I think I shall try and decline to be afraid.

Until I see my way a little clearer it is very difficult for me to write poetry or anything else.

I had a letter from Georg today. I think I shall come to Berlin to see him for 3 weeks or so in May; then I shall go to a cheap pension in the Salz Kammergut and try to work for two months. I really have a lot of work to do and have done quite a lot, but I am very dissatisfied with it and unwilling to show it to anyone. However, when I have six whole poems I will send them. They are very modest & even personal because I can't write pretensions any more (or I don't want to) even when the pretensions are not mine but those of something, like communism, which I believe in. I want to try and describe a phase of society with precision because when that phase is fully recognized people will want to go on to what grows out of it. Propaganda is external and deals with general statements which are the business of politicians I think. Poetry states something only by qualifying it and creating the circumstances in which it is true. I don't think poetry is useless because I think it can prepare people for political propaganda, and shake their prejudices.

Olive [Mangeot] & I are going to the *Bay Tree* on Friday. I'll send you a copy as soon as I can, when it is published.[27]

Jean [Ross][28] is very well & having an affair with a B.B.C. man. His wife asked her to sleep with him. His wife, like Hindenberg with Hitler, imagined that Jean's attraction would not last, but it has now lasted the amazingly long time of a month so she (the wife) is getting alarmed. Knowing that Jean is attracted by giants she has been giving her a series of tea parties for people not under 6ft 5 in order to seduce her from her husband.

I am going to see Richard [Crossman] this afternoon.

The mood of this letter is London.

Write to the above.

                                 Love, Stephen

What about *Sado?*

Love to J. Lehmann, & Heinz & Gerald [Hamilton].

LETTER 15

February 26 [1933]
43, Boundary Road
[London] N.W.8.[29]

Dear Christopher,

I write as I am very disturbed because I heard from a friend of mine in Spain that Hellmut has met you, so I'm afraid he has been making trouble. When I was first in Barcelona I told him the outlines of the circumstances of my leaving Berlin, partly to explain my presence [in Barcelona]. . . . [Later, when] Hellmut left Barcelona, he wrote [me] letters demanding explanations of such things as why Humphrey should have stayed on after *he* had left, and he also patronizingly consoled me about my ideals. He was now with a person called Erich Zacharias,[30] who was one of the people who had devoted himself to Hellmut, and I knew that all the time Hellmut had been with me he had been writing emotional letters to Erich Z., which were a kind of evasion of our problems [together] & which enabled him to play a double role (a) with me & (b) with Zacharias. Because I was determined that he shouldn't treat Zacharias [in the same way as he had me] I wrote & said I thought it was better we did not write to each other at all. For this reason and because he is the kind of person who cannot ever forgive anyone who has tried to help him I am sure that he detests me (in fact I believe he detests everyone) and the first sign I had of revenge was a letter from Georg influenced by Hellmut & with "Transport übernehmen Hellmut" written on the back.[31] I am extremely sorry I ever mentioned your name to him. . . . I apologize profoundly. I am so convinced—almost superstitiously—of his powers of malice that I hardly expect you to accept my apology if he has thought of something sufficiently evil to say or imply. I blame myself frightfully for ever having got myself into this position which is entirely my fault, but when I went to Barcelona I was very "erschüttert" by our row [mine and yours] and that is why I told him roughly about it.[32] If you are angry please write & let me know that you are angry so that I won't have to speculate as to the extent of the mischief. But do not be cutting or sarcastic about it—simply let me know. Because I have been amply rewarded already for ever trusting Hellmut. If he makes any accusations about our relationship in Barcelona please write to the people who were with us there & who write to him and are impartial. The address is: E. Tattersall, La Lista de Correos, Ibiza, Spain. He will probably tell you that I have made Chris Wood[33] break with him. This is also untrue. Chris & I took ten minutes to compare notes & found our experience with him was the same. Go on knowing Hellmut if you want to find out what his character is really like.

Michael & Erika [Spender] are married now & have been staying here. Humphrey is well. Olive [Mangeot] & I went to the *Green Bay Tree* together. I have had excellent reviews [of *Poems*]. I will send them when they are complete. Love to John [Lehmann].

Love, Stephen

LETTER 16

March 1 [1933]
43 Boundary Road
London, N.W.8.

Dear Christopher,
Thank you very much for your letter. I have been in bed four days

receiving purgatives of the most powerful kind every few hours and practically starving. So please excuse my writing as I am weak & am trembling with joy at your letter.

I had kept on worrying during the last few days lest we might have another estrangement. When I was first in Barcelona I was awfully upset about our quarrel & I could not get out of my head the letter you wrote me in London (I burnt this about 2 weeks ago, before I heard that you knew H[ellmut]). I did not feel better or anything but I had waves of feeling just the same & I used to wait for these times to write to you. Of course H saw these struggles going on, and of course I knew he might take advantage of it. He is very sensitive and I am sure I am not maligning him when I say he was intuitively jealous of our friendship from the first moment. Please do what you can for him. Perhaps you might cure him. What you say in your letter is quite true. Of course I signally failed, but the month when we were away together absolutely alone was successful, simply because then I was able to *hold* him. Directly I agreed to go back to Barcelona alone he had beaten me, and I was an idiot not to have realized this. You really might do something for him if you make him always deal directly with you.

As far as our (yours & my) friendship is concerned, it is not exactly that I want to be with you or see you very much. I mean I don't want to repeat former experiences. But you are the one person who *could* always understand me whether we are together or not, if you are willing to try. [Marston] is another, because he's the only other person who has seen me at my best & worst & yet trusts me completely. Of course, whatever happens, I shall go on living just in the same way, & I shall go on with my work, but if I felt you had abandoned the irritating, continual effort to love me & forgive me I would be very disappointed: in fact much more than that. You & [Marston] are the people I most like. For [Marston] everything is simple & there is no conflict. With you it is different, but in spite of everything you are always fighting & there is something very clear in my picture of you.

My tapeworm unfortunately won't quite leave me. The head is still there & with the head it will grow again. Otherwise I am perfectly fit. I really feel well now which is remarkable considering the very drastic treatment I have been having. If they don't find anything today I imagine they will give up for the time being.

The news from Germany is awful.[34] [deleted passage] No, perhaps I had better not say anything that might conceivably get you into trouble. Or is this a ridiculous fear?

Your letter was not at all patronizing. If this letter is absurd, you might try blaming my illness. But the feelings I want to express I have been thinking for days, & indeed I am sure they are the same as those I wrote when we were in London together. Love to Heinz whom I am glad you are always with. I am writing 3 stories & lots of poems. I am 24! I am coming out in May.

With Best Love, Stephen

Love to Georg if you see him. I suggested to John that I send *Light in August*.[35] Or have you read it? My address is always the same as I shall be home in a day or two I trust.[36]

LETTER 17

September 7 [1933]
28, Upper Montague Street
[London] N.W.1.

Dear Christopher,

I'm very sorry I never wrote to you, but we have not heard from you since we left Levanto,[37] and firstly I was vaguely waiting for your reply, and then more recently I was half-expecting you to come home.

Tony and I are both very well, though I had another attack from the worm which made me ill for a bit. We have been living in Humphrey's flat for the last few weeks and I have been working hard doing mostly reviews for various papers in order to try and earn £3 a week.[38] Tony helps me a lot with typing, and also he looks after the flat. We see quite a lot of people, mostly William [Plomer], Joe [Ackerley], and Gerald [Heard]. I have been writing a lot of poetry, but I never finish anything, because all my conclusions always strike me as false. So I've stopped publishing poems, and I don't think I will publish any for some time now.[39] Then in three years I may do a book called *Principles*.

In order to earn money I'm also doing a book for Cape about James.[40] Of course there is not much about James in it really: the frontpiece will be a lovely photo of him when he was 7 which I discovered, and the book will mostly be a discussion of his friendships with Boston lads between the ages of 7-17. I found out that when he was 40 he was castrated by an accident which happened to one of the earliest central heating radiators. The cover of my book is going to be a trellis of hot pipes with little jets of steam peeping out between them. Cape have given me £25, so they will be rather surprised, especially as they have to give me another £25 in receipt of the MS.

Rosamond [Lehmann] is going to have a baby in January. She is rather in retreat now, so we have not seen much of her recently. Francis Birrell has had a most terrible operation for an ulcer on the brain, and is slowly recovering from it. I nearly fainted when Gerald [Heard] described it to me this afternoon. John Lehmann is reported to be coming home in September. At the moment he is on various missions in Austria. Forster is very well, but there is a new law made by Trenchard that his policeman has to wear a bowler hat when visiting him. Tony Butts has rather disappeared into a world of Bantings and Gaythorne-Hardies & people whom I never see now.[41]

. . . I don't know what further news there is. I'm much as usual, feeling very low sometimes, then very high, as in Berlin. Tony and I talk much of you, because, as he says, you and Heinz are the only people "like us." Tony is longing to meet Heinz.

Apart from all this, the ship continues to sink, but I expect you read about this in your papers. Except for one's work and for one or two people, there seems nothing but rather futile and tepid amusements, so gradually I find I have to take more and more to working. I expect you'll find it the same when you come to London. I have given up wanting to be involved in anything important or big, but there are certain things I hate & others & people that I believe in, and everything I do is really just keeping up my end for things and people I do believe in, as far as I can.

Oh, I remember something. A friend of ours was in Berlin recently, and he says that everywhere you find communist leaflets & literature concealed in the cracks of walls. One day he was walking along the street & a procession of people singing the Red Flag was suddenly formed. As soon as the police arrived the procession had miraculously dissolved again into the crowd.

Wystan has taken to driving a car which he has bought, and the expense of which is also ruining him. So as he's blinder than ever you'd better hurry home if you want to see him before the worst happens. We went for a nice ride with him the other day and I said "you have to turn left here, Wystan." Later he said "but there was no branch road there," so I said, "yes, I only told you to turn left to avoid a fence you were going into."

There have been no very good shows lately. The usual plays, either very mildly funny, or else ingenious and slightly vicious, like "Dangerous Corner."[42] However, a Russian Ballet has been here which I've seen several times. It was very good and there were some new ones. In the Autumn you have some good films & the Old Vic to look forward to. There have been quite a lot of interesting books lately, but I forget what they were about. Ezra Pound has done some *XXX Cantos* which have some fine invective in them, but most of them are swathed & hidden beneath wrappings of scholarship à la Browning.[43] It is mostly rather like this:

> "Then that tough guy Julius Caesar
> Said to me
> 'Alexander you f------- cur
> Veni Vidi Vici'
> O il bello campo in autumno"

He is very familiar with the ancients, as Americans seem to like to be. He writes in French, Provençal, Spanish, German, Italian, Greek, & American. There is an excellent buggery story & a section devoted to politicians which is marvellously tonic.

I can't think of anything more to say. Love to you & Heinz.

Stephen

LETTER 18 _____

[January 1, 1934]
[London]

Dear Christopher,[44]

Here are my New Year wishes. When are you going away? Is it Friday?

New Year, 1934

> Here at the centre of the turning year,
> The turning Polar North,
> The frozen streets, and the black fiery joy
> Of the Child launched again forth,
> I ask that all the years and years
> Of future disappointment, like a snow

Chide me at one fall now.

I leave him who burns endlessly
In the brandy pudding crowned with holly,
And I ask that Time should freeze my skin
And all my fellow travellers harden
Who are not flattered by this town
Nor up its twenty storeys whirled
To prostitutes without infection.

Cloak us in accidents and in the failure
Of the high altar and marital adventure;
In family disgrace, denunciation
Of bankers, a premier's assassination.
From the government windows
Let heads of headlines watch depart,
Strangely depart by staying, those
Who build a new world in their heart.

Where scythe shall curve, but not upon our neck,
And lovers proceed to their forgetting work
Answering the harvests of obliteration.
After the frozen years and streets
Our tempered will shall plough across the nations.
This happy train that punishes no valley
This hand that moves to make the silent lines
Effect their beauty without robbery.

LETTER 19

September 14 [1934]
25, Randolph Crescent
London N.W.9.[45]

Dear Christopher,

I'm sorry not to have written for so long. Tony is sending you from London my poems in the new edition inscribed to you. I shall be home in four or five days and I then shall send you my new poem about Vienna.[46] I don't send it from here, because if they open things like that in the post, they seem to confiscate them. They don't often do so, but I don't want to risk my last copy. I want to know what you think of this poem as it is the longest & most explicit thing I've done.

William tells me your Ms. is with the Woolves;[47] that is very thrilling. Also, all the reviews I have seen of *Little Friend*[48] say how excellent the dialogue is. Congratulations.

We are going home now; in fact Tony has gone already. The reasons are chiefly financial, and now I've finished my books I'll have to do a few months' reviewing. Doctor's bills, dentists, etc. have been so expensive that I can't quite yet manage; although I have got in a much better position than we were in last year. But the move from Yugoslavia for Tony's operation[49] really did us down. I wish, like you, that we had been able to stay in one place all the summer. As it is, we could only be here by quite shamelessly living on Mrs. Gardiner, which we already have done for longer than I would care to say, but you can no doubt imagine. Anyhow she is much too nice a person to take advantage of. I wish you knew her, as she is the kind of person whom we were always hoping we were on the point of meeting in Berlin. She is altogether very sympathetic, and has undermined my morals in the few places that were uncorrupted. That is to say, I now drink, stay up all hours, etc.

The worst of our going back is that I don't see how we shall all ever meet. Muriel & Tony & I are thinking of going to Albania for a month in April, but I don't suppose we shall, and even if we do, it will only be in the nature of a holiday. Tony & I, in fact, are rather set on the idea of having a cottage in the English country, though my heart sinks when I think of it. However, I have now got to a stage when although I still want to see a few places in Europe, the thought of living anywhere seems equally unpleasant, so I imagine that means I shall just stay in some place where I am put. But I don't suppose I would be writing like this if it weren't for the miserable feeling of failure that returning to England always gives one.

By the way, when I send you the Ms., I'll also send you some [photos]. I took them the other day, for some unknown reason. Eigentlich they are only of Tony.

I quite agree with you about *Voyage au bout de la nuit*.[50] My line of its being a travel book was partly in reaction to Rosamond [Lehmann] who told me it was the most terrific novel she had ever read. . . .

Today I knew that I would write to you because I thought of the "du solltest nicht Hellmut sondern Dunkelmut heissen" joke.[51]

I am reading another of those Wells compendiums, called the

Science of Life.[52] It starts off with the huge assertion in black letters THE BODY IS A MACHINE, and then goes on to describe the bodies of Mr. Everyman, Mrs. Everywoman, and Mrs. Everymuse. Wells says that the human brain is absolutely marvellous, it is almost as complicated and has as many wires as the Central London Telephone Exchange. There are 100 yds of string in each of your testicles, and as much pipes as in the whole of the Inner Circle Tube in your intestine. He says that anyone who hasn't got a vagina beeping out of the back of the penis has no right to claim that he's homosexual, and a woman must show an incipient penis to pass as a Lesbian. Evolution is still progressing. I think Wells is the most superstitious writer living. Tony nearly fainted when he came to the chapter on the life of the ant.

You will have had quite enough of my comments on the political situation when you have read my poem.

I wish I could send you a nicer book. Have you read Laurens Van der Post's novel *In a Province?*[53] I would like to send you that. . . .

I have been thinking of you tenderly lately. I do wish we could meet. Perhaps in January, when I have settled up a lot of things, we shall be able to join you, or to propose something definite.[54]

Always your loving Stephen

Viele Liebe zu Heinz!

Write when you get the poem, called *Vienna.*

LETTER 20

Saturday
October 21 [1934]
25 Randolph Crescent
London W.9.[55]

Dear Christopher,

Thanks for your letter. Your flat sounds very nice in Copenhagen[56] but you sound slightly depressed. I hope it has passed over by now.

About the change. I don't feel in the least on a high horse about it; as a matter of fact, I absolutely agree with your saying that it is mostly a business of time, place and circumstance. It affects me so little that it has not even made any difference to my relationship with Tony. It has rather improved it on the whole. I think I am certainly fonder of him than I could be of any woman I know of. But as I find sleeping with a woman more satisfying, it also means that our relationship isn't something we tire of when we tire of it sexually. Anyhow, directly one writes about all this, one writes badly.

I am quite liking London. I see a lot of William [Plomer], and a fair amount of [Leo] Charlton,[57] Joe [Ackerley], Herbert Read, etc. etc. etc. etc., but as little as I can manage. The other evening we went to a meeting against the Sedition Bill.[58] Morgan [Forster], [J. B.] Priestley, the Bishop of Birmingham & Hannen Swaffer spoke. Morgan made much the best speech of the evening. He was beautifully eloquent, and at the same time personal, so that he had a kind of separate hold on each member of the audience. It's obviously a sort of example of their Greek spirit coming out—Morgan emerging as a kind of Pericles.

I send a copy of *The Spectator* with a review in it by me.[59] W[yndham] Lewis was so angry that he raged at the Editor for an hour about it. He now squares all the reviewers, and, of course, thought I was a safe enthusiast. It must have been a funny moment when he read the article. In this book he is rougher & more swaggering than ever, and Morgan is one of the people he contemptuously dismisses; personally, I would give all Lewis's works for *Howards End*,[60] so it rather annoyed me. The moral of the book was that there was no reason for any writer to exist except Wyndham Lewis. That is not a very new theme for him.

Tony has just come back from Wales, where he has been all this week.

Franz[61] is now in London with various members of the "bunch." He is bringing his latest to supper tomorrow night, but he has warned me not to expect anything quite up to the photographs he has shown us.

Greetings to my brother & sister-in-law.

Vielen grüssen: lieber Heinz.

Stephen und Tony

Hope you are well, Dear. Try and hop over to London some time. Congratulations on "Little Friend." I have seen it twice and think it is a beautiful film. Best love to you both.

Tony

Oh, about coming to Denmark. Humphrey is writing to say he may come out at Christmas. Try not to come to London in January, because I am going to Vienna then. If we have any money, Tony is going to join me on Feb. 1st, and we shall go for three weeks to Greece

Stephen Spender at Oxford, 1929 (Courtesy Humphrey Spender)

Heinz, Humphrey Spender and Christopher Isherwood at Sellin on
Insel Rügen, 1932 (Courtesy Humphrey Spender)

Stephen Spender in Berlin, 1933 (Courtesy Humphrey Spender)

Christopher Isherwood in his Berlin apartment, 1933
(Courtesy Humphrey Spender)

Unidentified Portuguese peasant and his son, Tony Hyndman, Christopher Isherwood, Heinz and Stephen Spender in Cintra, 1935 (Courtesy Humphrey Spender)

Tony Hyndman and Stephen Spender in Italy, 1936 (Courtesy Humphrey Spender)

W. H. Auden, Christopher Isherwood and Stephen Spender, 1936
(Courtesy Howard Carter)

Stephen Spender, 1939 (Courtesy Humphrey Spender)

via Trieste. This seems rather bad for our meeting. Can't you come over this Autumn, to see about your book?

Love to Paul.[62]

LETTER 21

[winter, 1934]
25 Randolph Crescent
London W.9.[63]

Dear Christopher,

I think the novel is really fearfully good. The character of Norris is quite complete, full-length, comic, and unforgettable. The technique is amazing. I am sure it will have a great success, even with reviewers.

I saw John Banting[64] yesterday, who said he was doing a cover for it. He also wondered whether you had any ideas for the cover. If so, will you tell him. His address is 33, Rochampton Lane, Putney, S.W.15.

You surely aren't going to change the title to *Mr. Norris Changes Trains?* *The Lost* is an excellent title; the other is arty.[65] *Portrait of Mr. Norris,* or just *Arthur Norris,* or *Portrait of a Spy*—anything would surely be better and less Hogarth Pressy. It gives one a sense of earrings. It is like *Fine Day for the Wedding,* or *The Postman Rings Twice.*

I'm afraid I don't know anyone in Barcelona. My times abroad are usually devoted to coping with one person. On this occasion it was Hellmut. The only people I did know there are now in Italy. I'm very sorry.

We are very busy. I do two or three reviews a week, and am at last really getting to the end of that book.[66] After I've finished it, I am going to completely rewrite *The Temple.*[67] I have a really good idea of it now, I think. I've really got more work than I can get through at present, which is a good thing, I suppose. I'll send you the revised *Vienna.* I expect I shall do it in Vienna in January. I ought to do the play but it always seems to get squashed under other things. Some short stories I would like to do.

The point about *The Temple* is that it is a legend. The characters must have no nationality, the scene must be invented as the book goes along, because it is their dream. What I realized in my new vision of this book is that the walk down the river represents an attempt to return to their childhood. Obviously, this must be contrasted with some sort of an attempt to have sex with a woman in Parts One & Two. It is the reaction from that. The hero must be the kind of person who has invented some external standard of criticism which is so real that everything he does seems fantasy. Like the Marxist criticism of bourgeois art. He must end the book by violently rejecting the whole world of fantasy. I think he must decide to take a job, perhaps to be the assistant to a factory inspector. That really exactly suits his social position: it fits him into the machine of wealth, work and Happiness.

My idea then was simply to have scenery of generalizations, abstractions not particulars, like this:

UNIVERSITY.

A BRIDGE connecting this with Ernest's house.

Ernest extracts the hero from the university, as one plucks leaves off a branch, or extracts a tooth.

ERNEST'S HOUSE.

THE TOWN WITH A LAKE IN THE MIDDLE, and so on. I hope this doesn't seem too "brainy" to you. It isn't at all to me, if you see my idea. The point is that the symbolic & the general aspect of everything must be heightened to such a degree that the whole thing becomes a worked-out dream.

Best love from Tony & me, Stephen

LETTER 22

January 18 [1935]
Vienna

Dear Christopher,

I am extremely sorry not to have written you for so long, but since December I have done a frightful lot of work. I rewrote my James book, which is now being printed, and here I have been writing reviews, an article, two poems and a short story which I began this morning.[68]

Muriel is just doing an examination in Histology. She's now half way through her medical course, and this autumn she will probably be able to take a patient for analysis. . . .

I think John [Lehmann]'s story is rather good, but introducing Rilke or someone as a kind of background seems to me rather an exaggerated way of justifying his hero's relationship with a boy whom he in any case never sees.

I am turning *Vienna* into a play. All the part that is in that poem is background, seen through the eyes of the three protagonists, who are, roughly, Tony, Muriel, & myself. The whole approach of the poem was direct in a sense that made it obscure. The conditions under which what I was describing was seen were all omitted, and without the poem being thus conditioned it had no foreground. I can't tell you how I repent about that.

The three stories are firstly an account of the death of an old man in the ward where Tony was ill; secondly, a socialist meeting in a country hut just after some children have been shot; thirdly, the story of that drunk person whom I met in Barcelona, the story called "To the Dead Islands."[69] This is the most difficult of the lot, as I have always thought a great deal about it. I think I shall have to do Muriel here. She will become the woman whom I "put on," when such a character is required. Though I think I could do one or two more now—eg. Winifred,[70] or Helen Gibb. But what I thought was that perhaps a rich, extremely generous & lively American woman is landed alone in Dubrovnik, having been left by her husband, perhaps vaguely like that American millionaire—John—whom we knew in Berlin. This young man then turns up in D. They have a great deal in common; he is very acute, sympathetic, talented even. They are also, as it were, exiles abroad. They both despise money & he helps himself to hers quite generously. She also has, from the beginning, the letters from Dr. Moehring about him, so she is vaguely uneasy. When he gets his attack she is not altogether surprised, but what does rather shock her is the extravagant generosity, the sort of other-worldliness with which she behaves, and at the same time that there is something *complete* about his prostration that makes her feel rather inferior. What I want then to show is that she realizes that this is a repetition of her life with her husband: at the same time she knows that it is not merely a repetition, because she had Moehring's letters, which show that his behavior is much more a whole way of life, which she herself passively accepts & assists. So that this is a crisis in her life, in which she decides definitely to let K[irk] go to the islands & do himself in. I want the picture of a healer who refuses to work a cure: a kind of saint on strike. Because that kind of idealism is a thing that may destroy itself I want to show a character at the moment when she sees that the virtue in her is destructive.

This is of course more interesting than the other stories; it is a kind of legend like the "Cactus" or "The Soldier's Disease," which I could never pull off.[71]

These legends grow & grow in one's mind. The longer one leaves them, it does not really matter. I have started sketching the opening scenes of *The Temple*, which I am going to call *The Liberal Cage* because it is an account of the completely free life possible to our time. But the play is far more necessary to me, as an exercise in technique, so I will do that first. I can leave *The Liberal Cage*. I shall do the stories, & make a little money.

On the back of the last sheet is a poem I wrote, the chorus from the play.

If Wystan is still there,[72] please tell him Tony wrote saying how much he & Gavin [Ewart] had enjoyed lunch with him, and also that Tony had explained to me what Wystan said about Malvern. It is perfectly all right; but I hope I shall see him when I get back, not at Malvern, as everything is such a rush there, and schools are rather disturbing to an insider. . . .

I don't feel a bit altered by my new life.[73] Please don't imagine so. Only a bit more confident about my work, & more & more absorbed in it, that is all really. I admire Tony & feel as I always did about him.

Best love to you & Heinz. Love to Michael & Erika.
Stephen[74]

Be warned now by the truthful sign
Which sleep struck on his mind.
Your loving dreamer will wake soon;
Denying then his soul's demand
With silenced years he'll thank your hand.

Only your love can prove as vast
As that unpeaceful sleeping sea
Which his terror does invest.
O dive there with a love as sure
As those waves threatening all the shore.

Beyond the day he's hid the night
The womb, where all the waters flow.
The human will is now a net
Catching the fish that gleam and fly,
Symbols by which he'll live or die.

The winged symbolic fish are words:
Such fish, that speak, you must obey.
Unbind the years from death's stiff weeds;
Show love his rival coursing by,
To silence fear's prodigious lie.

Imagination summons ghosts
To hunt the silent coast of dreams
But night's spectre, still unguessed,
Shakes our day with a loud drum
Saluting love & death that come.

Deny deny the world is black,
Build up the house to hide the tombs;
Those gathering waves you cannot block:
The house, the horse, the man are tame.
Love only, wins that losing game.[75]

LETTER 23

March 7 [1935]
25 Randolph Crescent
London W.9.[76]

Dear Christopher,

I am awfully sorry not to have written, but my life is very rushed these days, and I try to forget about the letters I should write. It is disgraceful though not to have written about your novel, which I enjoyed & go on enjoying enormously. You will know by now that it is highly praised in *The Telegraph*, & *The* [*New*] *Statesman*, & *The Spectator*, and nothing in the nocturnal sheet of your native provincial town.[77] The dear old Hogarth even fluttered out into a tremulous announcement, which, as I have eyes like microscopes for that sort of thing, I picked out of the garbage of the *Times Lit Sup*.

Since writing these lines, I have seen many reviews of your book, and several quite big advertisements. I also saw the Woolves last night, and Leonard told me that he had just arranged for a second printing.

I am terribly sorry for you and Heinz about this conscription.[78] I really couldn't believe that it would happen, for a long time at all events.

Leonard says now that a war is inevitable, as the world has got into the vicious rearmament circle of 1912.[79] Morgan also has given up hope of there being peace.

Why don't you go to America? I think I would immigrate now if I thought I would write about anything, if I were away from Europe. I somehow feel that you would be able to write there, perhaps even better than in England. However, as the war may start in America—with Japan—I suppose going away wouldn't necessarily help you.

Well, Tony and I are going to Austria over Germany, starting here on March 29th. We can't afford to get to Greece as I had hoped, because my money affairs still aren't going too well. So my idea is to stay for 14 days with Muriel in Vienna, and then, towards the end of April to move onto an Austrian lake. We can get rooms there quite cheaply & easily. Why don't you & Heinz join us in Austria, or Yugoslavia, sometime during the summer? We could easily stay away till Sept., if necessary.

During the summer, I am going to translate a large selection of Hölderlin's poems, as Edwin Muir and I are collaborating to do a vol. of them for Heinemann. Then I shall also do a vol. of short stories, for Faber.[80] I enclose a poem which is one of a series of four that I am doing.[81] I am working on two more, called A German Childhood and To Exiles. Then, when I have finished these studies, the Hölderlin poems, the stories, & The Destructive Element, I shall get to work on a novel which I told you about, an account of the kind of life possible to liberals, called "The Liberal Cage"; and the plays about European politics. I have a lot of sketches of parts of these books, but, you see, I haven't got the style, nor have I got the "tour de force" power of Wystan. Because, honestly, I don't think Wystan's terrific virtuosity quite compensates for his lack of a strong, lucid, objective, free-verse style. All that writing ballads, sonnets, blank verse, rhymed couplets, seems to me a kind of fire works which is marvellous of Wystan, but of no real help to anyone else writing poetry.

Now I've told you what I hope to do in these five years. I think all a writer can do—the only completely revolutionary attitude for him today—is to try and create standards which are really civilized. More like Blake & Hölderlin than Goethe & Browning-Tennyson, because B & H were not hirelings, but disinterested.

In a week I'll send you a proof of my book.[82] You needn't bother to return it. If you can't read it, because of all the goo or the corrections, throw it away, and in 6 weeks' time you'll get a proper copy. You may dislike the "brainy-little-chap" side of it, but all the same I think you'll see that it is important to me.

So you'll hear from me in a week from today.[83]

Love, Stephen

LETTER 24

June 10 [1935]

Pension Mlini

Mlini

Dubrovnik, Yugoslavia

Dear Christopher,

Thanks for your p[ost] c[ard] which has only taken 5 days to get here, though it has been over London and Vienna.

Look, I could certainly meet you in September, on my way back home. We are going to Venice in ten days, and thence to Innsbruck. We shall be in Austria till September, and then Tony will go to Vienna for two months, as he wants to learn German really well, and I shall go home. I can of course go home via Amsterdam or anywhere that you are. So I hope that you will be able to last out the summer before you decide to go to America. Anyhow, if you go to N. America, I shall be there in two year's time, I expect.[84] But do let's meet first in Europe. Tony will be very disappointed not to see you; in fact he will probably not want to go to Vienna. He is at the moment typing out some poems for you.

I like *The Dog Beneath the Skin* very much.[85] In fact it deserves superlative praise. The things I was least sure about were the speech of Sir Francis Crewe to the garden party when he says how different the world looks from underneath, how hypocritical everyone is, etc., and the exhortations of the chorus to people to act, without it being clear to me how they were supposed to act. But I shall read it again, and then I dare say it will be clear to me. As it is I suppose Wystan would deny that it has a message. The funny parts, a great deal of the satire, and the generous sweep of the whole theme, obsessive. Also the poetry is beautiful: it is really final & brilliant; the psychology is profound: except in the political satire; it is the politics I am most dubious about. However, it seems grudging to express anything but praise, because really it is an important work, which pushes most serious poetry & most novels completely into the background. I congratulate you on your share of it: I only regret that you cut out Low Vipend's speeches, but I suppose that was too irrelevant.

Really Wystan's work has in it an element of simplification & organic self-sufficiency. One is so swept away by it—at least I am— that for the moment one almost thinks that no other contemporary writing is necessary. For that reason, it is impossible to enter it without also adopting a critical attitude, and considering how far it gets. My feeling is that his psychology goes beyond analysis, & really states something: but his politics are ambivalent, brilliantly analytic, but they state nothing, except perhaps a certain violence. But this is only on a first reading.

Will you get the July *London Mercury,* price 1/-, I mean will your mother send it to you; it has a story of mine in it which I greatly want you to read.[86]

Will you send a line to reach me c/o Thos Cook, Venice, between July 21st & 26th? Franz is here.

Best love to you & Heinz, Stephen

LETTER 25

July 12 [1935]
Hotel Alte Post,
Mieders,
Stubaital, Innsbruck

Dear Christopher,

Thanks for your very generous remarks about my story. I am going on writing these stories now, in fact I am doing two at present. If I come to Amsterdam in September—i.e. if you are still there—I shall be able to bring you perhaps 3 stories, all of them a little longer than the present one. But I can't just stop writing poetry and devote myself to these stories, because I get so often stuck in them that they actually take weeks or months sometimes to write. I start one & get it to a certain stage and then have to put it aside till a time when I feel I can go on with it. Poetry, on the other hand, *means* much more to me than it ever did. Perhaps really, I rely too much on it, so that it is too personal and bears too much the weight of what I feel. I don't care whether people like my poems. What I think is that if people get interested in such subjects as exiles & the will & the ideas behind the poems, the poems will become clear. If they don't it really doesn't matter. The poems are not really sticky or obscure: it is their subjects and myself who are, I suppose, because they mean a tremendous lot to me.

Will you kindly send my story proofs here, for a few days, and then I will return them if you want them? I promised to let someone here read them.[87]

Tony will probably go home a few days earlier than I in August or September, so he would like to stay one or two days in Amsterdam round about August 27. Would this suit you? He wants to get a job, as really he hasn't enough to do now, and would rather have proper work, just as Heinz wants it. I shall be coming home about 14 days later, on Sept. 7th or 10th. Will you still be in Amsterdam then, do you think? I want most awfully to see you.

Do let me know whether you showed John [Lehmann] my story when he was in Amsterdam. I almost wrote asking you to do so, because I thought that you would do it better than anyone else. However, I thought that to write would be to give myself away rather. I wish I had been able to do the story without bringing him in. But the one fantastic & baroque aspect of his character was exactly the foreground I wanted, which put all the other characters into their proper positions. Of course, it is not a serious study of him. That would take a very long time.

Do you know Gisa [Soloweitschik]'s new name and address? I should like to write her, as I have heard nothing since she was married.

Humphrey [Spender] told me you were puzzled by a remark in a letter of mine in which I said, "I don't feel superior"; I think it must have been re. buggery.[88] It wasn't meant as a superior remark. It was only that you wrote to me saying you hoped I didn't feel superior, and that I wouldn't despise the old jokes we had together. So I merely remarked that I didn't, but it must have read stupidly. However, I may add that I would have no reason to feel superior in any case. . . .

There is really no news at all. I am working moderately hard, and reading a lot of Hölderlin. Winifred[89] is here and has to be taken up mountains occasionally. I always have a guilty feeling that I am not taking enough trouble over her, & so feel rather depressed. That explains this dull letter.

Remember the proofs & write soon, then I will try & write a better letter.

What work are you doing?

Greetings to Mr. Norris,[90] and love to Heinz.

from Stephen

LETTER 26[91]

August 1 [1935]
Gasthof Alte Post
Mieders
Stubaital, Innsbruck

My dear Christopher,

This is just a short note to let you know our plans. I shall be in Amsterdam somewhere about Sept. 1st, if that is all right for you. Tony is going home very soon now, from Vienna where he has been staying in Muriel's flat, but I don't expect he will go on to Amsterdam, because he says the fare is twice as much nearly as the direct fare. This will not be so expensive for me, because I shall get a reduction of 60%.

I am working very hard now, trying to get a volume of my short stories (only a small volume) ready by Autumn.[92] I am working on the longest of the stories now, and am not being altogether successful, but I hope that, in the long run, it will come out all right. The other stories are going to be "The Strange Death," "The Cactus," and a new one, called "The Third and a Half International." This will also be about Vienna and the groups of the S.P.D.[93] there.

Tony has decided to try to get a job. I expect he feels as Heinz does about not having one. He is seriously thinking of joining the Red Cross expedition to Abyssinia, for which they are enrolling volunteers. The only difficulty seems to be that he is on the Army Reserve, and I doubt if the Army will approve of his going. But I suppose that if the Red Cross want him enough, they will buy him out. It will be appalling work, but he says he has experience of the climate and also of soldiering, so it is certainly the sort of work he is cut out for, because he is also a very good nurse. If it is a choice between being a Bank Clerk and going into the Red Cross, perhaps he is right to choose the Red Cross.

There is really no more news. I asked Muriel about Heinz, and she said that if you were really willing to *buy* a citizenship for him, you could first of all get a lawyer to search for a suitable country.[94] She said that if he spent two days in a library for you, he would be able to provide full particulars, and you would be able to choose your country for H. She also said that you should be very careful about military service: that you do not get him patriated in some country where he will have to do it. America seems to be almost hopeless, unless he has already lived there for some years, and then is married to an American. I have asked her quite often about all this, and I am sure she has thought about it carefully, because she is really a generous and considerate person.

She was here for the day a few days ago, but is now in Yugoslavia. I shall not see her again for about a year, I am afraid.

Next spring I am going to have built a little working hut in the country, near to a cottage in Sussex that Humphrey and two friends of his have bought. Then when I want to write a book I shall go there, and not wander about having to work. When I go abroad I shall only go for a month or so, and shall be completely free.

J— has recovered from the shock about "The Strange Death." He wrote me [an angry] letter, which crossed one I had written to him, explaining I was going to change the character. . . . I'm afraid that I shall have to rewrite the whole thing. Also I had to send him your copy of the proofs, with my corrections on it, for his approval. I am very sorry about this, but I shall send you A. a copy of the *Mercury*, B. a copy of the whole book. As soon as I have finished my new story (the long one) I shall send it to you, but that may not be for another three weeks. Anyhow, I'll try to send it a few days before I get to Amsterdam.

I only saw two or three reviews of *The Dogskin*. It seems to have been unfairly reviewed. There was a foul one in *The Spectator*.[95] The critics are really disgraceful, because one would have thought that a chance to criticize you and Auden was worth taking seriously; but instead of that, they chose to pounce. I am looking forward to Olive [Mangeot]'s letter.

I am reading *Splendeurs et Misères des Courtisanes*. I wish you were here, because when I read those books in Germany, it was always so funny telling you about them. Also you could help me with the translation of Hölderlin, which is incredibly difficult. I am reading all I can of and about Hölderlin; he seems to me the most interesting of all Germans. There is a very good book about him and Kleist and Nietzsche by Stefan Zweig, called *Kampf mit dem Dämon*.[96]

The Destructive Element sold fairly well (about 1,000) and they have managed now to sell a few sheets of it to be bound up in America.[97]

Really, now I have told you all our news, so, with best love to you and Heinz,

Stephen

LETTER 27

November 14 [1935]
25 Randolph Crescent
[London] W.9

Dear Christopher,

I have not written, as I've been working hard, having finished "The Island" & done a story called "The Cousins." There is now only one more to do. I have frightful misgivings about "The Island"—but there it is. I had better finish this book & then get on with something else & not think at all about it. However, at the moment, I am in one of those awful moods of depression about my work, which completely undermine my confidence and make it impossible for me to do anything. If only I understood normal people—I keep on saying to myself: I am tied by every bind to the pathological. Don't reassure me though: I'll work again on Monday.

We'll be with you at the end of the month,[98] whether or not we let the flat. Now I think we'll leave here on the 29th or 30th. I myself will not get out of the train or plane, but will go on to Cologne for three or four days to see Curtius.[99] Do you mind hanging on for 3 or 4 days extra? The point is that I am very fond of him, and I don't know when I shall next get a chance to see him. Whenever in fact we travel, I try to put in a few days at Bonn, as that is the only way in which I can see Ernst Robert [Curtius].

If I can find it, I'll enclose the pamphlet about Portugal, with details of the boat which we'd take from Rotterdam.

Well, what it comes to is that next week I'll write a new ending to "The Dead Island." That is the only way to happiness!

Tony is immersed in politics. He is going to join the Party next week, I believe.[100] We're now on the verge of giving up this life in our flat & I'm very glad. Whenever we get back to England, I'll get an old car & do a tour of all the Industrial areas. That is like re-writing the end of the story: it offers a solution to the *problème de style*.

It is awful about the election. Nicolson is in as National Labour for Leicester. . . .

Oliver Baldwin is out, & so are lots of the strong candidates. It makes one quite sick.[101]

Well, best love, Stephen

Notes to Part Two

[1] Herbert Read, *Adelphi*, 5 (February, 1933), p. 379, and *Times Literary Supplement*, July 6, 1933, p. 463. Quoted in Hynes, *The Auden Generation*, pp. 98-9.

[2] This influence, according to Isherwood, was sometimes more than just theoretical and spiritual: *Poems* "also contained 'I think continually of those who were truly great . . . ,' which ends with what was to be one of Stephen's most quoted lines: 'And left the vivid air signed with their honour.' I find that I still want to boast of the fact that, when Stephen showed Christopher his original draft of this poem, it ended: 'And left the air signed with their vivid honour.' It was Christopher who urged the transposition of 'vivid'" (*CaHK*, p. 118).

[3] The second edition of *Poems*, published the following year, was dedicated to Christopher Isherwood.

[4] In *WWW*, Spender wrongly attributes the writing of this poem to 1935.

[5] Spender, *The Destructive Element* (London: Jonathan Cape, 1935), pp. 190-91.

[6] Robert Browning's "Home-Thoughts, From The Sea" appeared in *Dramatic Romances and Lyrics* (1845):

> Nobly, nobly Cape Saint Vincent to the North-west died away;
> Sunset ran, one glorious blood-red, reeking into Cadiz Bay;
> Bluish 'mid the burning water, full in face Trafalger lay;
> In the dimmest North-east distance dawned Gibraltar grand and gray;
>
> "Here and here did England help me: how can I help England?"—say
> Whoso turns as I, this evening, turn to God to praise and pray,
> While Jove's planet rises yonder, silent over Africa.

[7] Gerald Gould (1885-1936), poet and essayist, was an associate editor of the *Daily Herald* from 1919 to 1922, and later a regular reviewer for the *Observer*.

[8] According to Christopher Isherwood (in conversation with the editor), Georg was "a friend in Berlin."

[9] "Christopher borrowed some of William's mannerisms for the character called Peter Wilkinson in *Goodbye to Berlin*" (*CaHK*, p. 248).

[10] Spender had discovered Hemingway's work while at Oxford. This probably refers to *Death in the Afternoon,* published earlier in 1932.

[11] Unidentified friend.

[12] Lawrence's *Last Poems* was published in Florence in 1932, edited by R. Aldington and G. Orioli. According to *WWW,* "No attempt to resume Lawrence's ideas can explain the influence he had over me. . . . Besides opening my eyes to a world that was just not potential literature, he also seemed to challenge my own existence, my mind and my body" (p. 97).

[13] After studying music at the Yale School of Music, American composer Roger Sessions traveled extensively in Europe in the early thirties.

[14] This passage is quoted by Percy Lubbock in the introduction to his edition of *The Letters of Henry James* (New York, 1920).

[15] Knut Hamsun's *Pan* was published in 1894, translated into English under the same title in 1920.

[16] The dust-jacket blurb announced: "If Auden is the satirist of this poetical renaissance, Spender is its lyric poet." Hynes suggests the blurb was written by T. S. Eliot.

[17] Julien Green, American novelist born in Paris in 1900. His early fiction, written in French, has a hallucinatory quality and features characters in isolation.

[18] William Plomer's novel *Sado* had been published in 1931.

[19] "I will stick to my favourites," Isherwood had written. "The Port. Children who were rough. Oh young men. After they had tired. And, above all, The Pylons. The Pylons is the best thing in the book, I think" (*CaHK,* p. 118).

[20] *New Country: Prose and Poetry by the authors of New Signatures,* edited by Michael Roberts, was published in March, 1933. Spender's work apparently surfaced, as his essay "Poetry and Revolution" and the *four* poems, "The Morning Road," "After Success," "Alas, when he laughs," and "At the end of two months holiday," appear there.

[21] William Plomer's *Cecil Rhodes,* a biography of the British administrator and financier in South Africa (1853-1902), was published by Peter Davies in 1933.

[22] Joe Ackerley (1896-1967), English memoirist, dramatist, novelist, poet, and editor. A homosexual, Ackerley described his non-sexual

friendship with E. M. Forster as "the longest, closest, and most influential" of his life.

23 Earlier in January, the Anarchists and the Syndicalists began an uprising in Barcelona which was suppressed by Government forces.

24 Written on stationery imprinted with Spender's Frognal address: 10, Frognal—Hampstead, N.W.3. Tel. Hampstead 3137; a single line is drawn through 10, Frognal.

25 That is, Hitler's appointment as Chancellor of Germany on January 30, 1933.

26 G. W. Stonier argued in *The New Statesman and Nation*, 5 (February 4, 1933), p. 136, that *Poems* showed the influence of both Eliot and Lawrence. For other comment, see preface to Part Two.

27 *The Green Bay Tree*, a play by Mordaunt Shairp, was published by St. Martin's in 1933.

28 Isherwood based his character Sally Bowles in *Berlin Stories* on Jean Ross, whom he met in Berlin in 1931. "Jean was more essentially British than Sally; she grumbled like a true Englishwoman, with her grin-and-bear-it grin. And she was tougher. . . . Like Sally, she boasted continually about her lovers" (*CaHK*, p. 60).

29 Written on stationery imprinted with Spender's Frognal address. See Part Two, note 24.

30 Unidentified. *Erschüttert:* violently shaken; deeply affected.

31 The German seems meaningless; perhaps "Transport (of the letter) undertaken (by) Hellmut."

32 See preface to Part Two.

33 Friend and companion of Gerald Heard, Chris Wood "was about ten years younger than Gerald; handsome, shy but friendly, rich. . . . He also wrote short stories which showed considerable talent" (*CaHK*, p. 102).

34 The Reichstag fire on the night of February 27 had caused the immediate arrest of hundreds of anti-fascists. The deleted passage of about six words is made illegible by a heavy cross-out.

35 William Faulkner's novel *Light in August* had been published in October, 1932.

[36] Marginal comments.

[37] During their travels through Italy in the spring of 1933, Spender and Tony stayed for a time in Levanto.

[38] From April to December, 1933, Spender published five reviews (on books by Virginia Woolf, Harold Monro, Walter de la Mare, W. H. Dawson, Erich Roll, and John Middleton Murry) and an article, "Politics and Literature in 1933."

[39] Spender in fact only published four new poems in 1933 and one in 1934, including two translations of Rainer Maria Rilke.

[40] Expanded, this became *The Destructive Element*. In that book, Spender wrote that James "was called on as a volunteer to help with a fire engine to put out a bad fire. There was an accident, in which he was very seriously injured. . . . His attitude toward sex, whatever its origin, is important because it may also account for the prevalence of death as an ending to his stories. Castration, or the fear of castration, is supposed to preoccupy the mind with ideas of suicide and death." In a footnote, Spender continues, "The rumour of castration seems exaggerated and impossible" (pp. 36-7). Current scholarship holds that the injury was probably a slipped disc.

[41] John Banting designed many dust jackets for the Hogarth Press, including Isherwood's *The Memorial*. Francis Birrell, Tony Butts, and Gaythorne-Hardy were London acquaintances of Spender and Isherwood.

[42] *Dangerous Corner* by J. B. Priestley had opened on May 17, 1932, at the *Lyric* in London. It ran for 151 performances.

[43] Pound's *A Draft of XXX Cantos* was first published in 1930 by the Hours Press in Paris. It was published in England by Faber and Faber in 1933. The quote that follows does not appear in *The Cantos* and was written by Spender; the "excellent buggery story" appears in "Canto XII."

[44] Spender's greetings are written in ink below the poem, which is typed. The poem was first published in the second (revised) edition of *Poems* in September, 1934, under the title "New Year." In the published version, the last line reads "*Create* their beauty without robbery."

[45] Written in Vienna.

⁴⁶ *Vienna* (London: Faber and Faber, 1934). See preface to Part Two.

⁴⁷ *The Lost*, which was accepted and published by the Hogarth Press as *Mr. Norris Changes Trains* in 1935.

⁴⁸ Isherwood had been introduced to the German film director Berthold Viertel by Jean Ross. Viertel hired him to write a screenplay of Ernest Lothar's novel, *Kleine Freundin*, in collaboration with Margaret Kennedy. Although Kennedy's name appears above Isherwood's in the film's credits, the two writers never met as she withdrew from the project early on. The script of *Little Friend* was substantially Isherwood's.

⁴⁹ See preface to Part Two.

⁵⁰ Céline, *Voyage au bout de la nuit* (Paris: Librairie Gallimard, 1932).

⁵¹ "the 'you shouldn't be called Hellmut (high spirited) but Dunkelmut (dark spirited)' joke."

⁵² H. G. Wells, *The Science of Life: A Summary of Contemporary Knowledge about Life and its Possibilities* (London: Amalgamated Press, 1930).

⁵³ In Chapter XIV of *The Destructive Element* ("Upward, Kafka, and Van der Post"), Spender discusses *In a Province* as "a serious political novel which is a complete refutation of the revolutionary tactics of Communists . . . but which is not propagandist" (pp. 237, 250).

⁵⁴ Spender and Isherwood finally met the following August in Amsterdam.

⁵⁵ Written on stationery imprinted with the Randolph Crescent address.

⁵⁶ In early October, Isherwood and Heinz had travelled to Copenhagen. There they had met Michael and Erika Spender, who helped them locate a flat.

⁵⁷ According to Christopher Isherwood (in conversation with the editor), Leo Charlton was "a high ranking officer who resigned from the British Air Force to protest the bombing of some village somewhere."

⁵⁸ The "Incitement to Disaffection Bill," which would have made the

possession of anti-war literature an offense, was defeated after much debate.

⁵⁹ Spender's review of Wyndham Lewis' *Men Without Art*, "One Way Song," appeared in *The Spectator* (October 19, 1934), pp. 575-76: "Except in the first two chapters, this book is almost lacking in any serious critical appraisement of any writer. Apart from his vigorous enemy attack, in the name of satire and the great without, there seems almost no constructive side to Mr. Lewis's criticism." There is no mention of this review in Kulkarni's *Bibliography*.

⁶⁰ E. M. Forster's novel, *Howards End*, published in 1910.

⁶¹ Unidentified friend.

⁶² According to Christopher Isherwood (in conversation with the editor), "I think this was Paul Kryger, a Danish student who befriended Christopher and Heinz in Copenhagen and helped them in many ways."

⁶³ Written on stationery imprinted with the Randolph Crescent address.

⁶⁴ In *The Whispering Gallery*, John Lehmann recalled that "Leonard and Virginia Woolf had decided, after some hesitation, to publish *The Memorial*, and early in 1932 it came out in an unconventional brown-paper jacket designed by John Banting, one of the most original of many beautiful designs he did for the press to the delight of my friends and myself and the dismay of the booksellers."

⁶⁵ According to *CaHK*, when Isherwood "mailed the manuscript to the Hogarth Press, it was still called *The Lost*. But not long before its publication in 1935, he decided to alter its title to *Mr. Norris Changes Trains*. This, too, was a title which he had originally thought of in German: *Herr Norris Steigt Um*" (p. 188). In the American edition issued by William Morrow, the publisher persuaded Isherwood to change the title again, to *The Last of Mr. Norris*.

⁶⁶ *The Destructive Element*.

⁶⁷ Spender's unpublished novel written while an undergraduate. See Part One, note 2.

⁶⁸ Spender published three poems in the *London Mercury*, 32 (May, 1935), pp. 8-11 ("Elementary School Classroom," "At Night," and

"Exiles"), and "An English Woman in Austria," a review (p. 81). The short story is probably "Strange Death," published the following August in the *London Mercury*.

[69] Collected in *The Burning Cactus* (London: Faber and Faber, 1936) as "The Dead Islands."

[70] See Part Two, note 89.

[71] "The Burning Cactus" was first published in *Hound and Horn*, 7 (January–March, 1932), pp. 218-318. "The Soldier's Disease" was the first story Spender wrote; about 8,000 words long, it is unpublished.

[72] Auden had arrived in Copenhagen on January 10 to conclude work with Isherwood on their play *Where is Francis?* (*The Dog Beneath the Skin*).

[73] That is, his love affair with Muriel Gardiner. See preface to Part Two.

[74] The poem (or fragment) which follows was written on the last sheet of the letter.

[75] Unpublished.

[76] Written on Randolph Crescent stationery.

[77] William Plomer wrote of *Mr. Norris* in *The Spectator*, for example, that "It has value as a view of Berlin during the years preceding Hitler's triumph, and accordingly as a study of social disintegration and upheaval, and it has a deeper meaning than that, for it may be taken as a comment on the state of civilization in general during the last few years" (March 1, 1935, p. 346). About two weeks later, the *TLS* followed suit: "It is chiefly as a picture of Berlin just before the Nazi regime that the book is valuable" (March 14, 1935, p. 161).

[78] See preface to Part Two.

[79] Spender wrote in *WWW*, "Leonard and Virginia Woolf were among the few people in England who had a profound understanding of the state of the world in the 1930s; Leonard, because he was a political thinker and historian with an almost fatalistic understanding of the consequences of actions. . . . So that when, in 1934, I asked him whether he thought there would be a war, he replied: 'Yes, of course. Because when the nations enter the armaments race, as they are doing at the present, no other end is possible. The arms have to be used

before they become completely out of date'" (p. 154).

80 Spender in fact translated several poems by Hölderlin (see Letter 31), but the projected volume with Muir was never published. The volume of "short stories for Faber" became *The Burning Cactus.*

81 The manuscript is lost. "A German Childhood," if finished, remained unpublished; "To Exiles" was published as "Exiles" in the *London Mercury* (see Letter 22).

82 *The Destructive Element.*

83 If Spender included a note with the proof copy of his book, it has been lost.

84 Isherwood finally left for the United States (with Auden) on January 19, 1939; Spender made his first visit in 1947.

85 The play by Isherwood and Auden had been published by Faber in February.

86 "Strange Death," which actually appeared a month later than Spender expected, was published in August's *London Mercury.*

87 The proofs Spender refers to were probably of "The Strange Death."

88 See Letter 20.

89 According to Christopher Isherwood (in conversation with the editor), this was probably the companion hired by Spender's grandmother for the Spender children after the death of their father; she is called Caroline in *WWW.*

90 Gerald Hamilton. See "Major Figures in the Letters."

91 Typewritten.

92 *The Burning Cactus,* which finally included "The Dead Island," "The Cousins," "The Burning Cactus," "Two Deaths" ("The Strange Death"), and "By the Lake," was published by Faber and Faber in April, 1936.

93 The Austrian Social Democratic Party.

94 A year later, Isherwood hired Gerald Hamilton's lawyer to try and arrange Mexican citizenship for Heinz; the attempt was very expensive and unsuccessful.

[95] In "Poetry, Drama and Satire," a review of Eliot's *Murder in the Cathedral* and Isherwood and Auden's *The Dog Beneath the Skin* in *The Spectator*, 154 (June 28, 1935), pp. 1112-13, I. M. Parsons wrote that "In contrast to *Murder in the Cathedral*, *The Dog Beneath the Skin* is a shoddy affair, a half-baked little satire which gets nowhere. If it had been written by Mr. Brown and Mr. Smith, instead of by two intelligent young men like Mr. Auden and Mr. Isherwood, nobody would have bothered to publish it, and nobody would have been the loser. For of all the dreary jokes imaginable it must surely be the dreariest, the flattest, and the stalest that has managed to get into print for some time."

[96] Stefan Zweig's *Der Kampf mit dem Dämon: Hölderlin, Kleist, Nietzsche*, published in 1925, was volume two of his study *Die Baumeister der Welt*.

[97] *The Destructive Element* was published in America in 1936 by Houghton Mifflin Company.

[98] See preface to Part Two.

[99] Ernst Robert Curtius (1886-1956), German scholar, critic and philologist. In 1927, Curtius published a translation of Eliot's *The Waste Land* in German.

[100] According to *WWW*, Spender joined the Communist Party in the winter of 1936, Tony a short while later (pp. 210-12).

[101] Sir Harold Nicolson was National Liberal M.P. for West Leicester between 1935 and 1945. A biographer married to Victoria Sackville-West, Oliver Ridsdale Baldwin served as Labour M.P. for Dudley, 1929-31, and Paisley, 1945-47.

PART THREE

1936–1939

In mid-March, Spender and Tony left Isherwood and Heinz in Sintra, Portugal, for Spain. In *CaHK* Isherwood includes a passage from his diary: "It's all very friendly and we are perfectly pleasant about it, but of course we all know that our attempt at living here together has been a complete flop" (p. 234). Two days after Spender left Sintra, Auden arrived there and began working with Isherwood on their second play, *The Ascent of F6*. Over the next few months, Spender and Tony travelled from Barcelona to Greece and Austria, where Spender wrestled with the writing of his most thorough attempt to articulate his political philosophy:

> I have started writing a new version of my Gollancz book: I think I can do it now. It will be as I planned it, but will be written in a very different manner, like an imaginary autobiography without quotations—not like *The Element*, in any case. Anyhow, now I feel I am doing something like a prolonged newpaper article but as inventive as a story.
>
> (Letter 28)

This "imaginary autobiography" became Spender's central and most widely read prose work of the thirties, *Forward from Liberalism*.

The thirties in England was an era of political engagement, and Stephen Spender was a man of his time. As the Depression worsened and the shadow of Hitler lengthened over Europe, for many English intellectuals the political alternatives available became increasingly more circumscribed, until there seemed to be really only two— fascism or Communism. This was certainly the feeling of those who fought against Franco's Falangists in one of the most black-and-white of modern armed confrontations, the Spanish Civil War. Spender recalls in his autobiography that the thirties,

> which seemed so revolutionary, were in reality the end of a Liberal phase of history. They offered Liberal individualists their last chance to attach Liberal democracy to a people's cause: specifically, to the cause of Spanish democracy. The total armament of the civilized world drowned all individual efforts in a rising flood of mechanized power.
>
> (*WWW*, p. 290)

And as Liberal individualists (who under other circumstances would have had severe reservations about casting their lot with Marxism) found themselves being drowned in "the rising flood," many reached for the only life raft in sight—Communism. Spender had begun the decade as an essentially lyric poet who had some interest in politics; he ended it as the author of such politically oriented works as *Vienna, Forward from Liberalism,* and *Trial of a Judge,* as a contributor to *Left Review,* and, for a week at least, as a registered member of the Communist Party in England.

Spender's father was a staunch Liberal who believed that his party had brought prosperity and stability to the world. Political fringe groups, like the Communists and the Socialists, were, he felt, mere fanatics, while the Conservatives, with their attack on free trade, were no better. Yet these satisfactions conflicted with his son's yearnings for fulfillment in a world too well-ordered:

> When I was taught about the past, I often regretted that there were no great causes left to fight for; that I could not be crucified, nor go on a crusade, nor choose to defend the cause of Saint Joan against the (then) wicked English, nor free slaves nor kill tyrants. I thirsted for great injustices.
>
> (*WWW,* p. 2)

By the time Spender had reached Oxford, however, his vague desire to right "great injustices" had metamorphosed into a more specific goal—to become a writer of consequence. While Depression and fascism loomed on the horizon, it is not remarkable that Spender's letters from his Oxford years are concerned with topics—friendships, writing, undergraduate life—other than politics. The enemy was the stultifying atmosphere of the university, not social problems which were increasing in seriousness, and if one could only flee the university for someplace like Berlin to "do one's work" in peace, all would be well.

In the introduction to this volume I have already quoted Spender's statement that from 1931 onwards—1931 being the "watershed year" between two world wars with the Depression and the collapse of the second Labour Government in England, a revolution in Spain, and the Japanese invasion of Manchuria[1]*—he, like other members of his generation, began to focus his attention on the international situation. While he was at the university, Spender's poems (like the "Marston" sequence, for instance, and "My parents kept me from

---

*Notes to Part Three begin on p. 135.

children who were rough") were personal lyrics in the Romantic tradition, concerned with questions of love, time, and immortality:

> Never being, but always at the edge of Being,
> My head—Death Mask—is brought into the sun.
> With shadow pointing finger across cheek,
> I move lips for tasting, I move hands for touching,
> But never come nearer than touching
> Though Spirit lean outward for seeing.
> Observing rose, gold, eyes, an admired landscape,
> My senses record the act of wishing,
> Wishing to be
> Rose, gold, landscape or another.
> I claim fulfillment in the fact of loving.[2]

Yet, as I have already indicated, it was not these poems (which made up the first part of the 1933 *Poems*) which caught the reviewer's eyes, but rather the poems of "social consciousness," like "Moving through the silent crowd," "The Prisoners," and "Perhaps." These poems were written in 1931 and 1932, after the poet had left the university and was spending much of his time in Germany. Clearly, his emergence into Berlin life—"the poverty, the agitation, the propaganda witnessed by us in the streets and cafes" (*WWW*, pp. 129-30)—and, alternately, his months spent in Depression England, gave him a glimpse of life set against his father's notion of Liberal-produced well-being.

Although Spender's letter to Isherwood in February, 1933 (Letter 14) remarks that Communism is something he "believes in," Spender's political and social awareness at this time seems to have been simply a general concern for mankind, akin to his "thirst" for some cause to fight for. The poems of this period serve no particular political *cause*, but rather show a lyric poet's growing engagement with the general plight of the poor, the unemployed, the oppressed. When Edward Upward, Isherwood's close friend from childhood, joined the Communist Party, for example, Spender decided that (primarily because of his belief in the freedom of the individual) he himself could not embrace Marxism. And tellingly enough, his 1932-33 trip to Spain produced in the letters to Isherwood only the after-the-fact comment that "Barcelona is certainly the most red-hot revolutionary place I have ever been in," followed by the confession that "as I knew nothing about Spanish politics I really didn't get very thrilled: not nearly so much as in Berlin" (Letter 13). While as Herbert Read commented, the work in *Poems* demonstrated a sensibility "conscious of his social heritage of chaos and despair,"[3] the letters would indicate that political matters weighed less heavily on the young poet's mind than either domestic problems or his attempt at the "literary life."

Yet a transformation was taking place. By September, 1933, Spender was at work on *The Destructive Element*, and as he progressed the work slowly broadened its emphasis from a purely biographical or critical study of Henry James. "The idea for a book on James," Spender wrote in the preface, "gradually resolved itself, then, in my mind, into a book about modern writers and beliefs, or unbeliefs" (p. 13). This change in emphasis probably had two causes, one public, the other private. On January 30, 1933, Hitler had been appointed Chancellor of Germany, and the events which followed, leading up to the defeat of the anti-fascist Austrian Social Democrats in February of 1934, certainly had an effect on him. Also, his love affair with Muriel Gardiner must have had an impact; a political activist, she had given her apartment in Vienna and her money over to the cause of the Social Democrats. It was not long after the two had met that Spender set aside his prose study to write his sympathetic account of the Socialist struggle during the February Uprising, his long poem *Vienna*. When he returned to *The Destructive Element* (he told Isherwood in the letter of January 18, 1935, that he had rewritten his book), it is not really amazing that it was with an increased awareness of, and interest in, politics and the function of the writer in the world.

In his essay "Poetry and Revolution,"[4] Spender had written that while the artist must reflect a social consciousness, he must always be careful of being led "astray into practical politics." While *The Destructive Element* was a political statement as much as it was a work of criticism, it did not move far beyond the general attitude which informed *Poems;* although in it Spender did solidify his position of a kind of socialist humanism. "This book is not written in defense of any particular set of beliefs," he stated in the preface. Rather, it was a defense of the artist's need "to connect his life again with political life and influence it" (p. 19). Here, for Spender, "political life" was synonymous with "moral life," and it was that which provided the subject for the most important art. Recent public events, he argued, like revolutions and the Depression, "remain the most serious subject for our literature"; these events "are bound eventually to become absorbed into the tradition of literature; they are going to be the Figure in the Carpet" (p. 19). And perhaps most interesting, given his autobiographical themes of many of the Oxford poems and stories, was his insistence on the priority of the public over the personal:

> I think the predominance of autobiographical themes especially in fiction, is a sign of the neglect of subject matter, if not of the decadence of style. I am not saying that writers should not write in any particular way or according to anyone's direction, but at times it seems that the political movements of the time have a much greater moral significance than the life of the individual, and, indeed, the chief peculiarity of the individual is that his acts are morally unrelated to the political movement: such a time is present, and my attempt in this book is to turn the reader's and writer's attention outwards from himself to the world.
>
> (p. 205)

Yet, Spender argued, it did not follow that a political subject matter implied any sort of programmatic way of viewing the world. The artist must at all costs tell the truth—it was here that James, and to a lesser extent, Yeats, Joyce, Pound, and Eliot had succeeded; and it was here that Communist writers had, for the most part, failed. While the Modernists, Spender wrote, attempted to move further and further in their art to a presentation not of surface but of the objective truth below the surface, and in that attempt produced a great and true art, Communist writers had put their art at the service of a particular political scheme imposed from outside. James repeated again and again that he had no opinions; Communist writers had nothing but opinions, and all their ideology demanded of them was that they should be in their work "good and explicit exponents of Communism" (p. 254). The major drawback of Communist literature, Spender concluded, was not its subject matter; in fact, in the world of 1935, that was its greatest virtue. Edward Upward's short story "Sunday" and Van der Post's novel *In a Province* were, for example, important modern works precisely because they had taken revolutionary politics as their subject. Communist literature's great failing was that it permitted only a single interpretation of its subject, and that interpretation was based not on the artist's insight but on the Party's vision of the nature of the class struggle.

It was for that reason that Spender took exception to a manifesto which had appeared in the *Left Review* proposing that in its early stages the magazine "carry on rigorous criticism of all high-browism, intellectualism, abstract rationalism, and similar dilettantism."[5] "And what do these abusive terms mean?" Spender asked. "The answer is only too simple: it is everything that WE happen not to agree with ideologically" (p. 233). In February, 1933, Spender had written Isherwood that "propaganda is external and deals with general statements which are the business of politicians I think. Poetry states something only by qualifying it and creating the circumstances in which it is true" (Letter 14). Two years later, with the publication of *The Destructive Element,* his position had not altered; regardless of how sympathetic he was to many of the Communists' aims, Spender refused to diminish the necessary freedom of individual thought.

While *The Destructive Element* was essentially a work of literary criticism with political overtones, *Forward from Liberalism* was devoted entirely to the political question. We know from the letters that Spender had begun writing his "Gollancz book" by March, 1936; its working title was *Approach to Communism* and it was finished by July of the same year and published in January, 1937, by Gollancz under the amended title.

Spender is not a systematic philosopher, yet the book is fairly articulate. In the preface, he explains that *Forward from Liberalism* is "a personal book, in no sense the interpretation of the accepted views of any political party" (p. vii), though with a general application for others in his "position":

> I suppose I must call them liberals. By liberals I mean those who care for freedom more than for the privileges which have given freedom of intellect to individuals of one particular class; those who are prepared to work towards a classless society, if they are convinced that freedom will be enlarged in this way.
>
> (p. viii)

The book is then divided into three "journeys." In the first, "Journey Through Time," Spender attempts to analyse the failure of liberal idealism in history—a failure he sees as having been brought about by liberalism's inability to "prove to democracy that freedom was an economic reality" (p. 67) by allowing political rights to be undermined by the doctrine of *laissez faire* capitalism. In the second, "The Inner Journey," Spender asks questions which have occurred to him about the relationship between liberal idealism and Communism; he attempts to answer them, concluding that he is a Communist because he is a liberal who has "a regard for objective truth, an active will toward political justice" (p. 190). Finally, in "The Means and the Ends," Spender argues that the system of Communist Party cells "provides a deeper and far more effective discipline than Party dogma," and is the only form of organization that will elude the "fascist gunmen" (pp. 223-25). The only alternative to the success of the cell and, by extension, international socialism, he believes, is war. But if Communism triumphs, it will be "founded on a realistic basis of economic freedom," giving "the political choice of the individual will, within the limits of Communist morality" (p. 249) a far wider range than in capitalist countries. The result will be utopian: "the ideas of liberalism will materialize: no one will challenge the principle of freedom, and the individual shall have the right to work, leisure and every form of self-expression which does not interfere with his neighbour's happiness" (p. 249).

On his return to London from Europe in the fall of 1936, Spender had decided to separate from Tony, who got an apartment of his own and eventually a job working for the *Left Review*. Spender had gotten a letter from Muriel telling him that she was going to marry an Austrian worker who was the leader of her socialist group. He says in *WWW* that this came as no real surprise to him, and there is no mention of it in his letters to Isherwood, but he did seem to immerse himself in political causes, enlisting himself "as one of what Nevinson calls the great 'stage army of the good' who turn up at every political meeting and travel about the country giving little talks, subscribe to things, do free articles, etc." (Letter 35). And it was while speaking for an Aid-to-Spain meeting that he met Inez Pearn, the woman he would in just three weeks marry:

> It is difficult at this distance of time to understand why I did this. I certainly felt strongly attracted and this made me suspect that if I did not marry her quickly someone else would. I hated living alone, and was in a state of reaction after ending my love affair with Elizabeth. But these in themselves seem inadequate reasons for my getting married. . . . Perhaps, though, I was forced to act because I had reached that stage where work is not enough to fill the emptiness of living alone, friends had failed, and therefore marriage seemed the only solution.
>
> (*WWW*, p. 205)

Soon after Spender's marriage, *Forward from Liberalism* was published; the reaction among Communists, as Hynes points out, was mixed. Harold Laski saw the book as providing for the liberal members of the Left Book Club "the very great service of making them see what the choices are this generation has to make." In his study Spender had, however, questioned the proceedings of the Moscow trials, and many took offense; the *Daily Worker* wrote that it was "clear that Spender had not come very far 'Forward from Liberalism,'" while the *Labour Monthly* reported that the book was "completely wrong in many important and fundamental aspects of Communist policy."[6] Harry Pollitt, the Secretary of the British Communist Party, asked Spender to join the Party, assuring him that his membership would help the cause of the Spanish Republicans. Spender did, on Pollitt's agreement that he be allowed to disagree with Party dogma on certain points, although he recanted his criticism of the Moscow trials in an article which subsequently appeared in the *Daily Worker.* He was given a Party membership card, but as he explains in *WWW* "never paid or was asked to pay any Party dues" (p. 211). His single act as a member of the Party was to travel to Spain with Cuthbert Worsley to report on the sinking of the Russian ship *Comsomol* for the *Daily Worker,* a task he took on probably as much to expiate a feeling of guilt as anything else. For a few weeks before, Tony had left to fight in the war in Spain; Spender blamed the severing of their relationship and his own marriage for Tony's going.

Isherwood and Auden's collaboration, *The Ascent of F6,* had been published in late 1936 by Faber and Faber, and it opened at the Mercury Theatre on February 26, 1937, under the direction of Rupert Doone. The play got mixed reviews. Spender liked it, but felt that it suffered in comparison with either author's own work; Day Lewis wrote that the implications of the play were "at best Oxford group and at worst Fascist."[7] Throughout 1936 and early 1937, Isherwood's chief preoccupation had been the welfare of Heinz. Now, on May 12, after Isherwood had returned to Brussels following the production of *F6,* Heinz was expelled from Luxembourg and arrested by German officials for attempting to change his nationality and elude the draft. In June he went to trial and was sentenced to six months in prison and a year of labor service plus two years in the Army. Isherwood spent the summer completing the first volume of his autobiography, *Lions and Shadows,* which he had begun in 1933, and working with Auden on their play *On the Frontier.* He couldn't get over losing Heinz, however, and in October-November recorded in his diary that "Heinz is always the last person I think of at night, the first in the morning. Never to forget Heinz. Never to cease to be grateful to him for every moment of our five years together" (*CaHK*, p. 289). In the summer of 1937, Faber and Faber had offered Auden and Isherwood a contract to write a book about any Asian country they chose to visit, and on January 19, 1938, the pair left London for China. They would remain in the Orient for three and a half months, a trip which would occasion their collaboration on *Journey to a War.*

Spender returned to Spain in the summer of 1937 to attend the Writer's Congress in Madrid, carrying a forged passport provided by André Maurois. The purpose of the Congress was two-fold: publicly, the point was to discuss the Spanish Civil War; privately, the Conference provided a confrontation between the Stalinists and André Gide.

> For Gide had just published his famous *Retour de l'U.R.S.S.* in which he had made a detached and critical account of his impressions of a tour of Russia. . . . Far more sensational than the book itself was the fury with which it was received by the Communists. Gide who, only a few weeks previously, had been hailed in the Communist Press as the greatest living French writer come to salute the Workers' Republic, became overnight a "Fascist monster," "a self-confessed decadent bourgeois," and worse. The Writers' Conference was divided over the issue of Gide.
>
> (*WWW*, p. 241)

Spender had attended the Congress with high hopes for helping the Republican cause; he returned rather disillusioned over the atmosphere of "a Spoiled Children's Party" which prevailed there.

In the fall of 1937, Spender and Inez travelled to Devonshire so that he might recover from a minor operation, then returned to London where, for a time, Spender entered psychoanalysis. They lived first in Hammersmith then in Bloomsbury, where Spender tried to finish his play *Trial of a Judge*, a tragedy which traces the decline of a judge who falls because his liberalism cannot overcome the power of evil. Throughout 1938, Spender's marriage was in trouble; he continued to see Tony occasionally (the year before Spender had brought pressure on the Republican Army to return Tony to England), and Inez began an affair. Spender's collection of poems, *The Still Centre*, was published in March, 1939, by Faber and Faber, and was dedicated to Inez; the volume marked his disillusionment with politics and a return to the personal mode. The same month, the Spanish Civil War ended with the surrender of the Republicans in Madrid. Isherwood and Auden had left England for America on January 19th, and now, in July, Inez left Spender. Shortly after, Spender learned that his sister-in-law Margaret was dying of cancer. As he nursed her, the German armies attacked Poland, and on September 3, 1939, England and France declared war on Germany.

LETTER 28

March 24 [1936]
c/o Thomas Cook
Barcelona

Dear Christopher,

It is pouring with rain, you will be glad to hear. Still, since we left you, we've had at least four fine days out of eight.

We have excellent rooms here, but unfortunately they are only free until the 1st April. There are only two boats from Marseilles (none from here): one on the 28th, the next on April 13th. So it looks as if we shall sail on the 28th, as we don't want to have to find & move into new rooms for 14 days only. Besides which, it is unlikely we wd. find such nice ones.

Barcelona is a very nice town, much nicer than Madrid. From the Plaza Catalana down to the harbour there is a very wide road with a broad central pavement, on which there is everyday a market of flowers, parrots, love birds, newspaper stalls, hor d'oeuvres kiosks. You can get the newspapers from London 30 hours late: i.e. at midday from the day before. There are wonderful cinemas, and the bookshops are the best I have ever seen. There are French & German bookshops & you can buy books of every other language. Spanish literature is so alive that there are special counters for new books in Castilian & Catalan, a great many of which are poetry, very nicely produced! The book you see on every kiosk—even the smallest—is a new *Anthologia de la Poesia Cataluña*. There are very good concerts. This afternoon I am going to hear Kraus conduct the Casals Orchestra playing the 9th Symphony. Restaurants are wonderful. Altogether I feel exceedingly sorry that you & Heinz didn't winter here two years ago.

I have started writing a new version of my Gollancz book:[8] I think I can do it now. It will be as I planned it, but will be written in a very different manner, like an imaginary autobiography without quotations—not like *The Element*, in any case. Anyhow, now I feel I am doing something not like a prolonged newspaper article but as inventive as a story.

How is Morgan? Thank you again for *Abinger Harvest*,[9] which I enjoyed very much. I think I liked the historical sketches most, the literary ones least. I really don't think he's very good on Eliot & Woolf. Perhaps the trouble partly is that some of the essays suffer from brevity more than the others. Still, I think his treatment of Eliot is almost too insulting; he seems to regard him too simply as a poor lunatic not responsible for his actions or opinions.

I am reading Gerald [Heard]'s book,[10] which is very interesting. I don't know whether you'll like it, but if I finish it before we leave here, I'll post it back to Sintra.

Since I began writing this, (a) our landlady has announced that she can keep us on after April 1st, (b) we have discovered that there is a boat from Marseilles on April 7th. So we will stay here another fortnight, which I am delighted about, especially as I am getting through a certain amount of work here. I shall also be able to see the British Consul now; if I get a chance I shall ask him about your question.

Let me know how much I owe you for the coal. I had forgotten to ask Faber to send you those books, but I have done so now. Thanks for forwarding the *New Statesman*. Don't bother though to forward it again, as we can get the new numbers here; we couldn't get that number, though. I didn't like the G. W. Stonier diary much. Literary competition for this week, what article in the *New Statesman* Spring Book Number does the following quotation come from: "The road was empty . . . except for an enormous flock of sheep, being driven from high pastures, in charge of deeply-tanned young men and boys of a startling, wild beauty"?[11] I give you three guesses.

I enclose two stamps for Heinz. I send them now because, if you look on the reverse, you will see they belong to a numbered series, so it is probably right to have one or two new ones. I shall stick one on the envelope, so it is stamped. If Heinz wants them all stamped, you will return them, & I shall send them back through the post again.

Heinz would love the market here. Yesterday we saw four cages adjoining each other, one of which held a monkey, another a parrot, a third a tortoise, a fourth two puppies. Mostly they sell birds. All the "shepherds" who sell the animals are deeply tanned and bursting with health. They wear splendid shorts.

Put this address down in your note book: Barcelona, Paseo de Gracia 99, Entre Solo 2. As if you ever come here, you could not do better than stay in this flat. I don't know the name of the landlady. It costs 2/6 a day for each of us here.

The weather is fine again & has been for two days. Hope it is as good in Sintra. Best love to all.

Stephen

LETTER 29

March 28 [1936]
As from c/o Thomas Cook & Son,
Athens
[Barcelona]

Dear Christopher,

I enclose a check for 2/2 which I reckon to be about what I owe you for the coal bill. Also I send you a poem,[12] which will show you what I feel about a bit of Barcelona, called really Barceloneta.

The tower hasn't exploded, nor is my heart pierced with more swords than usual. The only annoyance at the moment is the fearful noise of Barcelona which rocks our rooms, making it possible only to sleep between the hours of 2 & 7 in the morning, and very difficult to work at any time.

Tomorrow I shall get a German book for Heinz. Meanwhile, I have asked the consul about the marriage ceremony.[13] He says it is simply a matter of the pair signing their names in a book. He formally asks each in turn whether he or she is willing to marry, & they sign—that is all. Before the ceremony he rings up the German consul to ask whether it is all right: this is also a pure formality. However, the consul can refuse to perform the ceremony. The German consul here is apparently not a Nazi but a German-Swiss, who treats the whole thing as a joke.

The British consul who is very hospitable to me personally, is really very [biased] I am afraid. He talks about the Spanish as some people talk about "niggers," saying that they speak Latin, they are uneducated, quarrelsome monkeys, etc. He told me quite frankly that he wished Companys—now president of Cataluña—had been shot in

'34.[17] He thinks bull-fighting cruel & degraded, but he seriously said that he would approve of gladiatorial matches, if Catalans were set onto each other. He is very friendly to me and took me to four exhibitions, in order to prove how badly the Catalans paint. At one of them, he looked at a painting of a Spanish boy and said, "Typical! Sure to grow up to be a bloody Socialist or something." Spanish children are most demoralising, so he won't let his children mix with them. His whole conversation is a stream of bad-tempered invective against Spain. As the people here know quite well how he feels, it is a wonder he isn't lynched.

My Catalan friend Manent is very nice, gentle & kind. He has read me some modern Spanish poetry, particularly by Lorca. It is quite easy to understand & very beautiful, I think. Politics here & the artistic movements are very interesting and drive the consul to furious rhapsodies. The idea of a British Consul who talks about Pax Britannica, reads Latin & obviously imagines himself a Roman provincial governor, & who screams invective against the country in which he works, appeals to me as a theme I might write about some day. T sends love. We leave here on the 6th.

Best love to all from Stephen

LETTER 30[15]

April 2 [1936]
As from c/o Thomas Cook
Athens
[Barcelona]

Dear Christopher,

Your letter of three days ago arrived today. I got one other letter from you, for which I thanked you. *The Olive Field*[16] hasn't arrived, but I still have hopes. You must have sent it a long time ago, in fact a day after your letter which I received at least a week ago. However, don't bother; if it's lost, it's lost; I shall read it sometime. After this will you kindly forward everything to Athens, where we are going next week; we leave here on Monday. I also sent a book to Heinz about three days ago. I'm afraid it is a dull translation of Jack London, but I looked through all the books in the shop in vain. What I hope is that the books he now has will last him out till we get to Vienna (in about five weeks' time) and then we shall send him some more.

Meanwhile, the present one is a present from us, as we wanted to give him one; I'm afraid it is a wretched and "symbolic" gift. After this, I shall be most careful to send a bill, so please don't feel that we are putting you in an awkward position if you want some more books from Vienna or London. Ah, I also sent you a cheque for coal; also a poem with a bad ending which I shall rewrite in a few months' time; but I'll leave it as it is for the present. *The Burning Cactus* should be on its way from Faber. I'll write a note to Heinz tomorrow. I'm very sorry about the rabbits, of whom, I hope, one still survives.

We have really had a very enjoyable time here. There is a very charming Catalan writer called Maria Manent, who takes us about everywhere. Barcelona has some very interesting things, such as the mayoral palace and the most magnificent collection of what is called Romanesque Art, arranged in a wonderful gallery. Politics are also very interesting here; they sound very like Irish politics, with a perpetual struggle between the Castilians and the Catalans. Yesterday we saw Companys and several members of his cabinet, who looked very nice; they had just come out of prison, where they have been for the last eighteen months. I also see a good deal of the British Consul, . . . who collects round him representative members of the English Colony. These people talk about the Spaniards, and particularly the Catalans, as though they were Colonists talking about the natives. I think I told you how in the first conversation I had with him [the Consul] told me he thought Companys should have been executed in 1934. The other night I had dinner at the consulate. Typically, some guest takes up a magazine, looks at a photograph of a Spanish woman and says, "How like them! A pretty, sniggering face, with nothing whatsoever behind it." They told me how foul the Spanish food was, how lousy Spanish literature, how mean the Catalans were. At that I told them how generously Manent had behaved, so they said he must be trying to get something out of me. Then I told them how he had taken me to the office of a publisher here, and when I had remarked that I liked very much a book containing 150 photographs of Spain, the publisher had immediately given it to me. They just shrugged their shoulders and said "That kind of generosity is Oriental." The Consul now advises every tourist who writes him not to come to Spain; he tells one this with great satisfaction; it is supposed to be on account of the political situation, but it is very largely spite. The other evening he was assiduously spreading rumours about an approaching "Financial Crash." The various Merchants of Death who have their dinner with him say, "What Spain wants is a strong Government to the Right." We had a talk about the wisdom of lending money to Germany. Someone mentioned that the money would probably be fired back at us in the form of high explosives; a young business man replied, "Well you have to admit that money lent to Germany would be very good for Nickel Shares." I am beginning to understand now why some countries don't like their trade to be run by Foreign Capitalists.

I haven't done very much work during the last fortnight or so; in fact the work position is getting rather serious. It is possible even that we might have to go back with a cargo boat to London directly from Athens. However, Muriel has written today to say that there is a very good library in Vienna where I could get any books I want, so this rather improves matters. Our arrangements also depend a little on whether those girls keep our flat; we shall hear about that in a day or two. Yes, Spain has been rather expensive. Madrid particularly so, as the hotel Fedden[17] recommended was ruinous. We are going third class to Athens on the boat, in order to make up a bit.

The only work I have been doing is to try and learn a little Castilian. I think I told you how much I like what I can understand of the poems of Lorca. There is a very nice poem about the Guardia Civil,[18] which contains the following lines:

> Pasan, si quieren pasar,
> y ocultan en la cabeza
> una vaga astronomia
> de pistolas inconcretas.

They go where they want to go and they conceal in their heads a vague astronomy of inconcrete pistols. It is very beautiful. There are a lot of very good things like that I would like to understand better than I do at present. I don't know any idioms, nor can I understand the use of pronouns always.

Hugo[19] is very good on Spanish, I think.

I am so glad you are getting on well with the play.[20]

The Burning Cactus has a very pretty emblem on the cover, of a Burning Pineapple. I think I shall have it printed on all my books in future. William [Plomer] writes saying that he can't understand why I travel so much. I wrote him a page of explanations yesterday, but I think I shall tear it up.[21]

Tony and I unite in sending best love to all three of you & any livestock that is surviving. Did the pansies, peas, cornflower, cassia come up?

Stephen

April 6 [1936]
As from c/o Thomas Cook
Athens
[Barcelona]

Dear Wystan[22]

I think you are quite right to give up G.P.O. Films[23] and to give up London. Personally I feel very grateful that you have done so, as I have been wondering rather how you could combine such a racketeering life with writing your own poetry. For us, too, it is rather a problem where we should live; so far we have managed by having a place in London and then rushing away somewhere or to many places, when I could no longer stand it. However, we are giving up Randolph Crescent in the autumn, so rather a crisis will arrive then as to where we should live, and I don't know quite what we shall decide. The trouble about the *vie littéraire* in London is that one can only resist it by developing a mask; William Plomer has done this quite well, but I could not adopt an attitude of only seeing the "right people," and refusing to see people who wanted to see me because of my Art etc., without *becoming* as frozen-up as my behavior.

Spain is very nice, and Barcelona is strongly to be recommended. I like Spaniards, Spanish, and the politics are very interesting; as much so as those of any great country before a revolution.

I am glad you are getting on so well with the play. I have done about a third of one, but I have not got through much of either that or the political book since we left Portugal. I will start on it properly after we have been to Greece. I expect that if I had seen *Dogskin* I would have withdrawn the "bachelor's flat" remark. I have just got Tom Eliot's *Collected Poems*, which have several things I hadn't seen before called "Burnt Norton."[24] My first impression is that this is rather disappointing. There is too much of the

> What might have been is an abstraction
> Remaining a perpetual possibility
> Only in a world of speculation.
> What might have been and what has been

Point to one end, which is always present.

Somehow Eliot moves with a rather puzzled frown through Thoughts of this kind. Perhaps Yeats, Laura Riding and even [Edmund] Blunden can do this kind of pseudo-philosophic writing better. However, I must read it through several times again.

I couldn't read one particular line of your letter. Was it "if you hear of any jobs (?) like reviewing . . . I should be delighted"? If you meant anything of the sort, I shall try and look out. Why don't you try and be dramatic critic of The [New] Statesman or something of the sort? Or even an article on "Books of the Week"? Actually, I am sure you will have no difficulty in getting the work you want, though all those jobs are to some extent sordid. They are a process by which one converts oneself into a very inflated currency.

Tony sends love to all at Alecrim.[25]

Best love from Stephen

If I were you I think I would live on backing dozens at Estoril—and Number 17.[26] Let me know how you like the stories.

LETTER 31 _____

April 23 [1936]
c/o Thomas Cook
Athens
[Delphi]

Dear Christopher,

I was delighted to get your letter and to hear that the play is already finished. You won't be surprised to hear that I haven't added a word to the Ms since we left Sintra, but I have written two or three articles, have begun about six poems & finished two, and since I heard from you about the play I have sketched out most of the first quarter of the Gollancz book, which will need a lot of filling in.[27] I am rather pleased with the idea of that book now and hope to write two thirds of it in May, when we are going to an island called Skiros.

Really in a way the Tower may have burst because Greece has certainly been a great revelation to me; also doing the Gollancz book is having its effect, because in writing it I am formulating all sorts of ideas I have had for a long time, and when they are written down I shall be to some extent pinned down by them myself.

The only review I have had yet is one from the *Evening Standard* which said that my book was full of bad stories, pretentious and empty, and could be summed up as "unreal people in unreal situations." Humphrey says there was a rather sniffy review in the *Observer*. I also glanced at one in the *Times Literary Supplement*, which was respectful & perhaps even favorable, but it seemed to think that Hellmut ought not to have cried so much or shuddered at the touch of a woman. It said this was an impressionist poet's overwrought overstatement. In future, if I write about my acquaintances I shall obviously have to tone them down, to make them a bit more "real." I've decided that the novel about Humphrey's hair would be too unlike "life."[28]

Anyhow that book is over & done with. The fact is though that the reviewers will also dislike the play (as they did *Vienna*);[29] and the Gollancz book will be all wrong too. Still, I refuse to write a didactic book full of quotations; I am setting out deliberately to be scrappy.

We are now at Delphi & tomorrow we are going to a monastery in the hills. Delphi is wonderfully beautiful with cliffy mountains on either side of a deep valley running down to the island sea, & with eagles above soaring "in the circuit of heaven." To me being in Greece is like living in the world of Hölderlin's poetry, and I see & experience here what were formerly only words in poetry to me. . . .

Is Wystan still with you?[30]

On Thursday we are going to Fronny [Turville-Petre]'s Island which is on the way to Skiros, where Rupert Brooke is buried.

Even Tony is very thrilled by Greece & is in his least materialistic mood. It is a pity we haven't got a *Baedeker* or some guide so as to have a faint idea what the various ruins & statues we see are. Tony also likes the park in Athens very much. He will write in a day or two.

Here is another poem, a shorter one, about Hölderlin's old age. There is a poem by Hölderlin which my first two lines quote.[31]

> When I was young I woke gladly in the morning
> With the dew I grieved towards the close of day.
> Now when I rise I curse the white cascade
> That refreshes all roots, & wish my eyelids
> Were dead shutters pushed down by the endless weight
> Of a mineral world. How strange it is that at evening
> When prolonged shadows lie down like cut hay
> In my mad age I rejoice and my soul sings

Burning vividly in the exact centre of a cold sky.

I am writing a poem that rhymes: but it will take me a long time to think of them; "reflect" & "reject" are all I've thought of so far. Also I've done 20 lines of "A Letter to W. H. Auden, Pedagogue."[32] It is quite good, I think.

How is Alfred?[33]

Also I translated part of a poem by Lorca. If I can get it corrected I'll send it to you as it's really very beautiful.

Best Love, Stephen

LETTER 32[34]

May 27 [1936]
Bei Lehmann
Invalidenstrasse 5
(*Atelier*)
Vienna III

Dear Christopher,

I was very glad to get your long letter, forwarded from Athens this morning. I'm very glad everything is going so well. I can imagine the hen house and the ducks in their pond. Today I discovered, amongst my photos, an old one of Teddy which made me feel quite sentimental.

The chief reason I haven't written is that I have been unwell with a fever contracted in Greece. Nevertheless hardly a day has passed in which I haven't contemplated a letter about Fronny's island and decided I would make an even worse hash of it than I am making of *Approach to Communism.* The illness seems to have disappeared without being defined, but I am having a blood test made, and shall know in a day or two what was or still may be wrong with me. If I am ill, it has turned into one of those illnesses throughout which one feels quite well.

We went to Saint Nicholas about a fortnight ago. Fronny has such a bad reputation in Athens that when I was out to tea with the daughters of my godfather . . . and I happened to mention that we are going to an island near Chalcis, quite a hush fell on the room. Then someone remarked that to say one was going to an island near Chalcis was like saying one was going to a city within the city of

Rome to see the wearer of a certain papal crown. Then I was told a lot of gossip about Francis, such as his ill-treatment of Erwin,[35] his meanness, the drink, his rudeness to everyone he meets in Athens, etc. As far as I can make out, the worst thing he did was to invite two young men to stay with him for three days; and, on the third day, when they announced they were going by the 3.30 train to Athens, they waited till 3 for lunch, when Fronny announced that he was afraid none could be got ready so quickly. I tried to stop the rot by mentioning that there was another side to the Erwin story, but it was no use. When I said how charming I thought Fronny was, people just looked at me as reviewers must at my works when they say the situations are Unreal.

On the day when we arrived we were late, as accidently we got into a part of the train which was going to Thebes. So we arrived at the island at 4 o'clock, just in time for an early lunch. Fronny was very drunk indeed and swayed about a great deal and repeated himself a lot telling stories about his guests. He was rather upset because two young men who had turned up the week before had been Buchmanites. When Fronny heard this, he pointed to Niko (photos enclosed), and said "I suppose you realize that that is my wife." Fronny wondered very much what they thought of him.

Niko is very pretty, and she has a genius for doing nothing except play with a string of beads all day. The rest of the household are a rather handsome cook and a little boy who pads into the room with bare feet to serve: he is the housemaid. Besides this there is a nice chauffeur, with a daughter, to whom Fronny is godfather, and all sorts of minor gardeners, etc. The servants are quite good at their jobs: Fronny has taught them to do everything except wash, with the result that the cook was about the dirtiest person I have ever seen. The house is now rather dark, as Fronny has had to close-in the verandah, which is one enormous cloud of flies. To get to the drinks (vide photo of Fronny and Tony), one has to fight one's way through the flies, which is most unpleasant.

Fronny now detests eating, and eats almost nothing. Meals are two, three, four hours late, whilst Fronny sits drinking Ouzo after Ouzo in order to nerve himself to take a bite of one tiny little fish or piece of meat which was divided amongst us. We had lunch at 3.30 or 4 most days, and dinner at 11, after the news on the wireless, which was at 10.30 p.m. One evening there was no reply. We looked into the kitchen and found they had both gone to sleep over the food.

Everything there is very inconsequential. Fronny told us not to breakfast with him, because he had breakfasted in bed at 7.30 a.m. "What do you do then?" I asked, impressed. "I go to sleep."

We went for an excursion to a neighbouring island which was completely barren. The Greek servants rushed about capturing hawks and seagull eggs. Then we ate charcoal-covered octopus—very tough. We went on a motor-boat which Fronny had just acquired. It is built, for some reason, in such a way that no one can sit down on it, as it consists simply of a long cabin eaved over with a high, pointed roof, like an ark. So we all went clinging as best we could to the roof, as though we were on an uncomfortable rubber serpent in a swimming bath, made with the sole object of overturning at any moment.

The island is very beautiful, I think. He has built a charming walled-in garden full of tropical flowers.

Fronny is very lonely, and mildly complained to me that none of his servants had ever heard of Homer, and that there was nothing to talk to anyone about. I see him now as a person with an absolute passion for Greece; he is one of the great Philhellenes of which there are a long and curious tradition. He is also, more obviously, of course a mediaeval saint, living in the intoxicating flies and mud and disease of his hermitage. But I had never realized before now how much he was a scholar, because I had no questions to ask about Greece in Berlin. He drank much less on the second and third days, and he talked a lot, mostly about Greece. He was very charming indeed, in a way that almost brings tears to my eyes. Naturally I felt annoyed with the people in Athens, though most of what they say about him is true, and in any case he doesn't care what they say. All the same, I have learnt something from the reviewers of my book: that people like the hero of "the Dead Island" and, in a different way, Fronny, can be dismissed as intolerable egotists. I can't help feeling that there is a certain justice in this, and I wonder why I never thought of this particular objection to them before.

Certainly there are people who seem to enjoy the life on Fronny's island. One was a young man who lived there for eighteen months; the other, a woman, an artist who stayed for eight months, and who is coming out again. Fronny seemed quite sentimental about her, which is odd. Personally, I was very interested, but I certainly wouldn't have cared to stay. Nor can I imagine how you and Heinz stuck it out.

Tony and I went back to Athens, then we went to one of the islands of the Cyclades, called Paros, where we intended to stay for a month.

This was most unpleasant. The people were so poor that they never smiled, and they regarded us with a concentrated intensity of surprise that we should want to come to a place so dirty as their island, which got on our nerves. Luckily my temperature got very high and it was absolutely necessary that I should see a doctor. The doctor put me on a diet of macaroni and toast and we came to Vienna by the Orient Express, which was after all cheaper than the Slav boats that crawl along the Dalmatian coast.

Here we stayed a few days with Muriel, and now are in John [Lehmann]'s flat, which is exceedingly swell. I write at a table beneath which is a line of eight drawers made of an excellent wood, and containing bits of *New Writing*.[36] In front of me is a wall map inlaid with maps framed in papier maché. The maps are of Europe, Asia, Austria, Leningrad (two, one general, with a figure of Lenin, the other more detailed of the centre of the town), Paris, the Vorarlberg, London, Budapest, Venice, Prague, Moscow, the Caucasus, Atter der Kammersee, another part of Austria, Linz, Innsbruck, Steyr, Graz, Semmering, and a huge one of Vienna. The desk where I am working is on a raised platform, three steps above the well of the room which is built into a tower, whose spacious windows command an enormous view of Vienna. There are many plants on the window sills, and there is a second table on the platform. In the well of the room there is a huge L-shaped mattress-sofa. Opposite the sofa a bedroom has been built-into the room from which it is curtained off. The room is clean and comfortable and excellent for work. . . . The kitchen by the way is frescoed with negroes shaking cocktails etc., the vorzimmer with various kinds of fish.

I am getting on with my work, though not with the play. The communist book oppresses me somewhat, and will till I have finished it, I suppose. Muriel is very busy and happy and I admire her way of life enormously.

John was nice and friendly when we saw him. He has now gone back to Fieldhead for the six weeks during which we have taken this flat.

On the reverse of this there is a poem.[37]

Best love from Tony and me to Heinz and you.

Thanks for what you say about my book and the reviews. I am not at all put off by what I have seen. I know B— slightly; he holds the Spite Record even in London. Gerald [Heard] is very interested in him because he has a chin which is growing longer and longer. Finally

Gerald says it will be covered with hairs such as those on a horse's tail, and will be kept in a wooden box, with a small trap door at the end, through which food can be shoved. Then Gerald will write a book about it, and there will be some photographs in the *Listener.* The book will be called This Expanding Universe: A Trilogy, vols. VI to IX of the What Gerald Heard series.

Stephen

LETTER 33

July 27 [1936]
Gasthof Hollbrau,
Salzburg
Judengasse

Dear Christopher and Heinz,

I am so sorry that neither of us have written for at least seven weeks, but in that time I have written at least as many ten thousands of words. Thank God, my book is now finished and I shall post it off to Gollancz tomorrow morning. So you will see that I am writing to you in my first free moment.

Perhaps we shall exchange this book for *The Ascent of F6,* which I see announced in Faber's catalogue? They are both record breakers as far as the speed in which they were written is concerned. I really think that this book will quite interest you too, and that I have avoided all the more obvious things. Of course, it is written in my usual shocking English, due to my not knowing one end of a sentence from the other. But I think that finally if I go on writing badly long enough, it will become one of my qualifications. Actually, some of it is quite effective, I think.

Now I am going to start writing the play again.[38] At once. I have learnt how to work hard during the past few months.

John has now come back so we have left his flat and spent the last few days at Sulz. On Monday (tomorrow) we are going for five days to a place called St. Wolfgang on a lake near Salzburg, in order to recover from the book. Then we are going to Salzburg, where I shall stay for ten days, Tony two, after which he will go home. I am going to Paris after Salzburg, in order to see a woman who is translating one or two of my stories. I may go away by myself for a few weeks after that to the coast of Brittany in order to finish my play; otherwise I shall go away to England later, I suppose.

During the past few weeks, Muriel and I and another friend have taken Spanish lessons, so that I know quite a bit now. I have discovered some very beautiful modern Spanish poetry, mostly by Garcia Lorca. I'm also going to read a play by Lopez, which is often performed in Russia, as it is about a peasant rising. I read a very good novel indeed, called *Seven Red Sundays*, by Ramon J. Sender.[39] Faber published it. You really ought to read it, as it gives one more an idea of modern Spain than anything else I have ever read. So much so, that everything I read in the papers now about Spain seems almost as though it were a sequel of that novel.

You never said what you thought of the *Olive Field*. I admired it very much, but somehow I never managed to get to the end of it. He is a very good and very careful and intelligent writer,[40] but I find him very dull.

Every day Muriel says that she is going to write and thank you for *Dogskin*, which she liked very much. Though I believe she enjoyed the *New Writing* story[41] better than anything else of yours. She spends every morning now assisting at big operations, and besides this she has a great deal of work to do, so I am sure you will understand that she is very bad at writing letters.

Gavin Ewart and John Madge have been staying at the cottage with us here for the last five days. They are both very nice, I think. I have taken what I hope will turn out to be some rather good photos of us all.

Tony went to a doctor a few weeks ago, who divulged that for the past four years, including some of the time he was in the army, he has had an ulcer of the stomach. He has now been x-rayed and tested, so it is proved beyond a doubt. He is on a rather strict diet, and has to rest for two hours every day with a flannel over his stomach. We have both given up smoking, which is really a very good thing to do, I believe. He is not allowed to drink either. I feel rather annoyed with all the other doctors who might have found this out years ago simply by making x-rays. However, it is not really serious, and he should be quite well by Christmas.

Moore [Crosthwaite][42] has turned up from Bagdad, and we are going to see him in Salzburg, where there is also a Casino. However, I think my gambling days are over, as I have never felt tempted to go to the one very near Vienna.

Everyone here expects that the Nazis will be in Vienna before another year, and after the first little wave of optimism, no one expects any good of this new pact.[43] However, there has been an amnesty in which they have let out a good many socialists, as well as the murderers of Dollfus.[44] The Nazis seem to be very divided; some of them have decided that they are betrayed against Hitler and are going to sabotage the pact; but whether they accept it or work against it, they will equally be playing into his hands. If the Nazis come, I must marry a woman here, who is also a friend of Viertel.[45]

We haven't heard the news from Spain yet, as it is impossible to get papers at Sulz. You can imagine what I feel about it. In fact I feel much more strongly than I ever did before about these things, as a result of having got my ideas down on paper.

When you read my book you will see that I don't take the view now that everything you and I—for example—care for, will be wiped out by C[ommunism]. I hope you will agree with my reasons for thinking differently about this, as it is an important point.

I often wonder about the hens and the progress of the Five Years' scheme in the garden. Did the young ones grow up all right? How many rabbits are there now? What is the weather like in Sintra? Sometimes I imagine a crisp wind blowing from the sea, sometimes your hill in clouds.

I have read *Eyeless in Gaza*[46] which is very interesting. He has some ideas now, but they are all wrong; a sort of half-religious, mystical pacifism. I do hope that Wystan doesn't fall for it. Just in case, I have tried to show it up in my book, where I have also attacked David Garnett, the *Daily Herald* and the Book Societies quite vigorously.[47] Rosamond has sent her book.[48] . . . The book certainly made me realize that I, at all events, am, by now, completely bigoted and shut off from most things that people mean by Life, and one certainly ought to be frank enough to realize that and own that perhaps one isn't capable of judging about people's love affairs any more.

Anyhow, I must write to Rosamond now, and say this, though in a different way.

Best love to Heinz and you, Stephen & Tony

LETTER 34

October 5 [1936]
As from 11, Queen's Mansions
Brook Green
London W.6.
[Suffolk]

Dear Christopher,

I was sorry to hear by various routes about Heinz's operation or—is it two?—operations. I hope that he is better now. The best of nose and mouth operations is that though they are painful, they are slight and usually lead to a spectacular improvement in one's general health.

You will probably have heard my news, but I'd better confirm it. The best is that Tony has a half-time job, working on the *Left Review*.[49] This is entirely due to the kindness and generosity of Derek.[50] He has now taken a small flat, in which Cuthbert [Worsley] has the use of a room when he comes up to town. The other half of the week he works for me; there is also the C[ommunist] P[arty] work, so he is rather busy. Tony, Cuthbert & I have taken a very small 3 room cottage in Suffolk for 10/- a week. It is very nice & easy to work here. I have also got a smaller & much nicer flat in London.[51] So Tony & I are now, as it were, semi-independent. As I have told you, I think this is good as an experiment at any rate. The job with the *Left Review* may come to nothing, but I & Cecil Day Lewis are trying to help by doing regular features for it so as to double its circulation. If it doesn't do that, I suppose Tony will lose his job. You will see then that if you can send a story or article to *Left Review*, several people will be even more grateful than is usual in such cases.[52]

Next, Gollancz have chosen my book for their Left Book Club. This means quite a lot of cash, as about 25,000 copies will be sold. I think I'll be able to send you a proof in a week's time.

About the *Ascent*. I liked it very much. It's impossible to say much more than this until I see it performed as all the points I am unclear about would either be cleared up or made defects by the acting. On a first reading, I was slightly disappointed because I judged it on the one hand by Wystan's single poems & on the other by your novels or stories. To me, it isn't as interesting as either but I dare say that is inherent in what you are trying to do. It strikes me that you both, as it were, draw too much on your ample resources. Wystan's psychology comes pat, the son is in love with his mother, there are lots of striking bits of annotation & psychological observation; this is a currency on which Wystan can draw whenever he likes. The same with characterization—your hallmark—which is altogether well done.

I think that probably a play is bound to be a display of "effects," so this is not criticism at all. I only say it to show my state of mind. Anyhow, there are very beautiful & interesting scenes, it is an improvement on *Dogskin*, and Ransom is very moving. I think Wystan's versification now has a light style of its own, which is quite distinct from jazz or doggerel.

When I have seen the performance, I shall know my mind. Louis MacNeice says you have re-written a lot, in which case I have no doubt that you will have removed my objections.

I have only read the play once. I may feel quite differently about it when I read it a second & third time.

I am struggling on with my play. After that I am going to write a novel about some English people in Barcelona who write me insulting letters from time to time. This will be very straight-forward and exciting—unlike what I have done up till now I think.

Please give my love & the enclosed to Heinz. No, I shall post a separate letter to him.

Love, Stephen

LETTER 35

October 30 [1936]
11 Queen's Mansions
Brook Green
[London] W.6.[53]

Dear Christopher,

Thank you very much for your letter which I was very pleased and touched by. What you say about my book is most generous and I am very grateful to you for saying it. For the rest, I think you exaggerate the contrast between our lives, but again I appreciate your sympathy in doing so. It is true that I am rapidly enlisting myself as one of what Nevinson calls the great "stage army of the good" who turn up at every political meeting and travel about the country giving little talks, subscribe to things, do free articles, etc. Actually this is only valuable to me as experience, and in that way I do think I get quite a lot out of it. But of course, it's stupid to pretend that it will have the slightest effect on anything;[54] whereas I still secretly and perhaps exaggeratedly believe that a very good book about things one cares for is a potent instrument. And imaginative work is more important than one more voice added to a controversial babel. So really, because I feel that wherever you go you always are, to a greater extent than I, in touch with what is going on around you, I don't really see that there is such a violent contrast. I just have to work rather hard to establish contacts which I imagine you have all the time, that is all. And as for the virtue of political work, I just can't judge about that: I just hope that it isn't so entirely useless as it seems on the surface. Anyhow, the great thing for me is that I am writing my play. That I do care about.

Of course, I rather wish you were here as a political asset. I am sure that you would be very good as a public speaker, for example. At present I am almost useless, but as long as people want me to do so, I think I'll go on trying. I can imagine you being very dynamic. And I recall that even in ordinary conversations you wave your arms about and have "gestures"; that is what I absolutely fail to do, unless falling over once and twisting my legs round each other into a knot counts.[55]

Anyway, I am going to accept requests to speak to the Birmingham University Socialists, at the Sunday *Times* Book Exhibition, for the Spanish Workers, etc., for the next six months. At the end of the winter I shall decide whether I am any good at doing this kind of thing. If not, I shall give it up; though I think I'll accept an invitation to go on a lecture tour to the U.S.A. next year,[56] as it should be interesting.

I'll send you today or tomorrow *Left Review* with my article on the *Ascent*, which you may not have seen.[57] When it actually comes on, one of us will write it up again to do it the justice it deserves.[58] I hope you won't feel I've been unfair. Really my only objection is that at the end of the play instead of giving the *consequences* of Ransom being the kind of person he is, you give an acute piece of analysis. To my mind the most interesting thing about Ransom is that he is a prig; perhaps that is even more important than his fascism, which is after all a doctrinaire point. I am sure it is more important than that he is in love with his mother. I can't help taking it for granted that all Wystan's & your heroes are in love with their mothers.

An American friend of mine, called Lincoln Kirstein,[59] wrote to me how much he admired the *Ascent* which seems to be very successful over there.

I have written about ⅓ of the third & longest scene of my play and I think it is good. I'm not sure when it will be ready but I don't really see why I shouldn't take as long as I choose over it. There are so many jobs I have to hurry over that it is lovely to have something which I can work over again & again & think about a great deal. It thrills me to write this kind of poetry, which is very clear, & which, in all the different characters, expresses all the divisions in my own mind.

Cuthbert & I have a small cottage in the country where I have been working the last four or five days. Erica [Spender] calls it a rat-ridden hole & says 10/- a week is far too much for it. . . . There is a lot to tell you that I don't want to write in a letter, because it doesn't in the least concern myself & in fact is just gossip.

Tony is very busy with *Left Review* but still works for me about two days a week. The C[ommunist] P[arty] are amazingly exacting, but I dare say that it is a good thing. I am afraid that if I joined I would have almost no time in which to write; there is too little time already. Tony has a very small flat in London; but for the next week or so he will stay with me, because Herbert List has turned up in London & has nowhere to stay and can get no money.[60] There has been a clean-up in Hamburg & he is afraid to go back until it's all blown over; perhaps he will never go back. Now if I went to Hamburg, he would certainly put me up; but then he would go to work each morning, so it wouldn't matter my being in his studio. In a rash moment of conscientious generosity, I said he could stay with me indefinitely; then I realized that since he has nothing to do in London & I have only one large living room, this was madness, so I have beaten the only possible retreat, which is to let him have Tony's flat. You know how meanly one feels on these occasions, but I am beginning to find that if one wants to write books one has to behave meanly and even dishonestly with people. It is a form of egotism with me that if someone makes a request of my time—that I should meet him or attend some meeting—I feel the most absolute sense of obligation; I feel that people can't exist without me. Also, I sometimes feel at the very mercy of people—that I cannot refuse any request they make; I now think that this is a [way] of being at the mercy of one's own feelings if one sympathizes with [the people concerned], or even if we dislike them. These things seem very unimportant but they form the drama of London.

I look forward very much to seeing you if the *Ascent* is performed. If it isn't, shall I come over to Brussels sometime in December or early January? I would really like that, and I might combine it with a few days at Bonn. But possibly you prefer people not to come to Brussels; anyhow, let me know what you prefer.

I do hope Heinz is well again now. Actually the only operations I really believe in are tonsils & nose operations; usually they result in the most spectacular improvement in one's health. I was ill for several years intermittently until I had my tonsils out; & have scarcely been a day in bed since.

Please give my love to Heinz & yourself.

Stephen

LETTER 36

November 22 [1936]
11 Queen's Mansions
Brook Green
[London] W.6.[61]

Dear Christopher,

This letter is just to reaffirm what Tony will have told you already, that I am going to be married. The girl is called Inez Pearn and she is very nice indeed and I am in love with her, and, I think, she with me. It is useless to say any more at present, because you will meet her either when you come to London or if we go over to Brussels next year. I'm afraid though that I shall have to put off going to Brussels for Christmas.

Tony is very upset indeed, sometimes accepting it, and sometimes being furious. He has just made the most terrific scene; perhaps though that isn't a bad thing as on the whole it seems to cheer him up a bit to say whatever is most on his mind. I think that . . . after he has a flat of his own and a job and a lover, it won't make such a difference to him as he thinks. If I wasn't married, however, I couldn't go on seeing him supposing I tried simply to have an affair with Inez; because he would make it quite impossible for me to have any relationship with her: I would all the time be having a much more dynamic one of scenes and reconciliations with him.

This is not why I am marrying; a whole lot of things go to make an absolutely final step necessary. I'm just not capable any more of having "affairs" with people; they are simply a part of a general addiction to sexual adventures. She also wants to marry me, and I think that we shall be able to build up a satisfactory life together. I am sure that you will understand this necessity for a permanent and established relationship, because I know that you have always felt it so strongly yourself.

The fact is that I feel exactly the same as I have for a very long time about Tony. If he will accept himself as my best friend rather than lover, on the basis of his independent life and job, things will be all right. It is certainly far more difficult for him than for me, but I do hope that he doesn't insist on his present position which really is that although we have stopped living together I mustn't live with anyone else, particularly not a woman. Because that will destroy our relationship completely. I can't make my marriage a sort of function of my friendship with him, because that isn't how I feel about it.

Apart from this worry, I feel very happy indeed and this has solved a lot of things for me. I have felt lately that my personal life was bound to become more and more sterile, because the complete dependence of Tony was destructive to both of us, and there was nothing else even when I tried to alter that.

I can't write about Inez because you don't know her, but I think you will like her. She's the only girl I've ever met[62]—no, it's no use trying to write about it. You will have to meet her though. If I write, it is like trying to force my view of her on to you and that will just make a false start for your meeting.

Who should I meet today in the foyer of Faber & Faber than Miss Pearce, carrying a large portfolio under her arm! She explained to me that it contained my spirit portrait, which she was trying to sell to Eliot as a possible frontpiece to my next book. I let it go, feeling pretty sure that they wouldn't buy it. During our brief encounter I didn't have time to discover whether she had become a member of the firm of Mitchell, Peter and Portugese exiles, masseuses to Mrs. Simpson.[63]

I also had lunch with Michael [Spender] and Gerald Heard; Michael was determined to keep the meal to one subject, entitled Science and the Popular front. . . . He talked a great deal about the Position of Women in the Fascist State, which he seemed to think was not based entirely on unreason. When he heard about my marriage, he coughed and said, "Get to know all you can about the girl's parents. That is a very important biological point." As a matter of fact, Inez had been educated all her life in convents, a French and an English one: but she has lapsed. Her great interest is Spain and Spanish, which also are the only two knowledgeable things which I would really care to learn about.

I'm afraid this letter is rather a muddle, but I spend my time alternatively feeling very happy and very worried. With best love to you and Heinz.

Stephen

LETTER 37 ————————————————————————————

November 25 [1936]
11 Queen's Mansions
Brook Green
[London] W.6.

Dear Xtopher,

This is just a postscript to my letter of two days ago, which was rather over-agitated, I think. Anyhow, everything is going quite well now and Tony has become much more reconciled to the idea of our marriage. It is very unpleasant for him, but if he manages not to mind so much about the unpleasantness of taking second place, our friendship won't be so awfully different from what it has already been for a good time; so I hope.

What I most wanted to write to you about is that Inez & I shall probably be coming to Brussels in the middle of January, for two months. If we don't do so, she will lose her travelling scholarship: it seems to me eight weeks in Brussels is quite worth £100. My idea is to finish my play during that 8 weeks, besides going on with my *Left Review* articles & other work.

If you are there, it will be very nice as I imagine us having those pleasant dinners together. I am almost sure that you will like Inez, and that Heinz will also. We want to do quite a lot of skating during the winter. Do you think we could get a little flat, with a small kitchen and 2 or 3 rooms? Whilst I am in Brussels I shall really work very hard indeed, as it will be a great chance to do so.

Should you think my marriage may embarass you in any way, it needn't at all impinge on you. Still, it will be very pleasant to know that Heinz & you are there & that we can occasionally have meals together. Do let me know how you feel about it.

Wystan was here last night & read his *Byron Letter*,[64] which is much the best piece of political writing & the most enjoyable stuff he has done.

If you would really like T[ony] still to come out at Christmas, with

Cuthbert, it would be most awfully nice of you to write him a line to say so.

With love to you & Heinz from Stephen

LETTER 38

December 27 [1936]
11 Queen's Mansions
Brook Green
[London] W.6.[65]

Dear Xtopher,

Thank you very much for your letter; thank Heinz also for his greetings.

I look forward to hearing from you tomorrow or the next day.

Meanwhile I quite agree that the most important thing is we all get to know each other. Inez & I will arrive about Jan. 20th. Could you look out for some place where we could stay, suitable for me to work & both of us to have meals? She will be working at the library.

I hope you will agree that Giles[66] is really awfully nice. I got very fond of him during the past few months.

I get appalling nausea about their going,[67] when I am tired. But it is fairly clear to me that I should finish my play before I make another move, & that I think I shall do. The reporting idea seems to me a good one.

I can't help hoping that there will be a military coup in Germany during the next months? But I suppose that is blind optimism.

Humphrey photographed the baby.

Best New Year greetings to you both.

Stephen

LETTER 39

[c. December 30, 1936]
11 Queen's Mansions
Brook Green
[London] W.6.[68]

Dear Christopher,

Thank you for your letter, which I am very grateful for.

I am very glad you have the same impression as I did about Tony's motives for going away. Once, about a month ago, when I did think he was going on account of our marriage, I dissuaded him. But this time I didn't try to do so, because I felt, as he did, that he was particularly well qualified to go. . . .

It is true, I dare say, that if we had lived together here & not separately, he might not have gone to Spain, because to a great extent I atrophied his power of making independent decisions. From our rows and occasional outbursts of his, I know this made him more deeply miserable than even the most rash decision could do. Therefore I come back & back to the point that I had to make this external break, although it was the most difficult decision I have ever made.

Apart from this, the question of responsibility is a matter for other people not for me to decide. All I know is that I love him & that whenever he comes back, I shall be extremely happy and that I wish he were now here, and that I miss him very much. His sister thinks it is the fault of my ideas that he has gone to Spain; she is quite right from her point of view: but from mine, such arguments don't apply: only what I feel directly does.

I think you will like Inez very much, when we all meet. I would rather be with you than with anyone in London now because you will understand these matters, and nothing else at the moment seems very important to me, except my work & the general business about Spain.

I don't write about Inez because you don't know her yet. Nor would I have been able to write about Tony, if you hadn't met him already and realized how he and I still feel about each other.

We shall arrive on the 20th of January. Does that suit you? I have to talk to a Left Book Club Centre on the 19th.

Best love, Stephen

Thank you very much from us both for the sherry which will be most useful.

We all rather fell in love with Giles during the last few weeks: he was so very nice.

LETTER 40

January 5 [1937]
As from Gibraltar[69]

Dearest Christopher,

Cuthbert & I are going for 14 days on rather an important job to the rebel part of Spain. We shall[70] go to Cadiz & probably Burgos. I shall tell you all about it when Inez & I reach Brussels.[71]

Since Tony went, I have felt frightfully unhappy and this feeling has grown worse, on account of all the news in the papers. There is nothing really to say about it, except that this job will probably restore my balance a bit.

Inez is at home, where I shall join her before we leave for Brussels.

If Wystan[72] is with you, give him my love. Apart from this awful business Inez & I are well & quite all right. Only it does undermine everything. I am going through what I think of as your Danish Winter. I also get colitis & shit blood—only not so much, I expect.

Please thank Heinz for his nice card & ask him to forgive me for not writing. . . .

All the best, S.

LETTER 41

February 20, 1937
Gerona[73]

Dear Christopher,

I was very touched by your last few words to me. It wasn't so much what [Cyril] Connolly said that depressed me as the feeling that the spirit in which he said it—a careless and profound and inexcusable cruelty—suddenly seemed almost universal.[74] These people have a horrible way of making their own apprehensions seem the most *final* attitude of mind possible. Of course really it is their passion to make their own attitude of mind seem fashionable. His *New Statesmen* article is utterly destructive—and stupid, I believe.

Love S.

LETTER 42

August 3 [1939]
[Suffolk]

Dear Christopher,
I have been meaning to write to you for a long time. Thank you meanwhile for your letter which I have left in London, so I cannot remember whether there were any particular things in it I wanted to answer.

The reason I haven't written is because this year I have been feeling more and more apprehensive about the appalling disaster that has now happened to me. Inez has left me and decided to go live with M—. . . . There is no real quarrel between us and I am sure I shall love her and she me in the way in which I love, say, you and Wystan. In the long run, this will doubtless be a comfort, but in the short run it makes things far worse, because it means that a person whom I really love and with whom I have every chance of being happy for a long time, has decided that living with me is too difficult because I feel things too strongly, worry too much, have too much personality for her to feel independent, etc. . . . I have always loved people in the manner of thinking that they were indispensable to me and of becoming completely absorbed in their personalities. So perhaps this terrible lesson is necessary, and I shall be able to learn something from it which I have always been afraid to learn: depending on myself, and being prepared to accept my own isolation. Anyhow, I feel that I shall have to work better, because there is nothing else for me to do. I am going to cut myself off for six months from her, and at the same time ask her not to decide what she really wants until the end of that time. I'll go to Paris for some time, and stay at a cheap hotel and write my books. I'll try not to upset anyone else's life, and generally lead a more self-respecting and even happier kind of life. Perhaps when I can endure my own life without making other people suffer and pay for it, I shall be fit to live with someone, and she may even want to live with me then, though of course I cannot count on or even expect that. Meanwhile I've simply got to get through the next few weeks as best I can. I'm sure it will be all right. And perhaps it is wrong to have a relationship in which one is so absolutely entranced by someone that one is always hoping that she will come into the room, and one never gets tired of the novelty of seeing her. Inez has some absolutely unique quality for me which I can't imagine in anyone else—but perhaps that is unhealthy. Perhaps I can even learn to love her in a more detached kind of way.

I do wish you were in London, as then I could talk to you, and you would be a great comfort to me. I am awfully sorry about all your troubles too. I know there was a good deal of talk about it and I thought you'd probably done something slightly crazy which I would not like but which can't make any difference towards my attitude to you. In fact, nothing could do that, although I am quite capable of thinking very realistically about people I love. One reason I didn't write to you is because I thought you'd thought that I was a violent militarist or something from one letter you wrote, so I didn't think it was any use trying to explain how utterly fed up I am with politics and any kind of public life, though I suppose one has to do a certain amount. However, I am now acquitted for six months, I suppose.

If there is a war, I think I'll probably do just what I'm told to do, even to the extent of joining up. This isn't a militarist attitude; it is really one of feeling that the time when one can do anything against these nationalist machines has now passed, and the only thing to do is to accept the dictates of what I think to be the slightly better side. I thoroughly sympathize with your point of view, however, and I even rather envy you it. At the moment I simply cannot understand the motives of high politics. I know it's stupid to write like this, but in a way I have learned something when I realize that what I most wanted out of life was to write my own stuff and to have a satisfactory relation with Inez. I only imagined I wanted a lot of other things; and I can't even understand very well what people like Hitler want. Or, if I do understand, I can't relate my activity to theirs except by allowing them to put me into a totally false position in which I am joining the C[ommunist] P[arty], making public speeches, sitting on committees, etc.

All one can do is learn a very little within a very limited sphere of interest, so surely one ought to limit one's aims to what one can cope with, and try to see that one does not take revenge on the people around one for what one has got from life oneself. If one does this, one has a chance of learning one's lessons without having to justify one's existence to too large an audience. One has to look on everything in life as experience, and imagine one is in a kind of purgatory where humiliations are not just humiliations which one has to justify and cover over, but opportunities to go back and make up for some earlier mistake from which one is recovering. Everything one writes, if one is a writer, is just a record of one's mistakes in living, and one has to accept this, and gradually learn, and gradually extract a little comfort from things, and gradually forgive oneself. Being an artist . . . is just a kind of disease of suffering. It gives one the kind of unfair advantage over one's contemporaries in history which people who accumulate large fortunes have. But the only thing worth having is the power to make people happy and the willingness to be ignored and forgotten. Men of genius are only parasites on those who have the real gift of entering into happy relations with their fellow-beings. They are feeding all the time on life, and if there weren't people who have an equal intensity of experience in life itself, there would be no audience for the creations of the artists.

I won't go on any more. I'll send you one or two poems I've done recently. THE AMBITIOUS SON[75] is unfinished because Inez's letter came just when I had got to that point, and I haven't been able to go on. But I dare say I'll finish it later.

Please give my love to Gerald [Hamilton]. Write to me again c/o the Hogarth Press.

Best love, Stephen

Notes to Part Three

[1] Hynes, p. 65.

[2] Collected in *Poems*.

[3] See Part Two, note 1.

[4] In *New Country*, ed. by Michael Roberts (London: The Hogarth Press, 1933).

[5] Alec Brown, "Controversy: Writers' International," *Left Review* (December, 1934), p. 76.

[6] J. R. Campbell, "Forward from Liberalism—but Whither?", *Daily Worker*, February 1, 1937; Harry Pollitt, "Liberalism and Communism," *Labour Monthly*, 19 (March, 1937), p. 188. Quoted in Hynes, pp. 262-63.

[7] C. Day Lewis, "Paging Mankind," *Poetry*, 49 (January, 1937), p. 227.

[8] Spender's *Forward from Liberalism*, published by Gollancz in January, 1937, was announced the previous October under the title *Approach to Communism*.

[9] E. M. Forster's *Abinger Harvest*, published in London by Edward Arnold & Co. earlier in the year, contained essays and sketches on "The Present," "Books," "The Past," and "The East," as well as "The Abinger Pageant," a masque. In his short piece on T. S. Eliot, Forster concludes that Eliot "is difficult because he has seen something terrible, and (underestimating, I think, the general decency of his audience) has declined to say so plainly."

[10] Probably Heard's *These Hurrying Years*, published earlier in 1934.

[11] John Lehmann, "Caucasian Note," *The New Statesman and Nation*, 11 (March 14, 1936), p. 381.

[12] The manuscript has been lost; however, this was probably "Town Shore at Barcelona," which was published in *The New Statesman and Nation*, 11 (April 11, 1936), p. 566.

[13] Probably a reference to another of Isherwood's schemes for helping Heinz elude German military service.

[14] Luis Companys, President of Cataluña and leader of the Catalan Left-Liberal Party, the Esquerra.

[15] Typewritten.

[16] Ralph Bates' *The Olive Field* (London: Jonathan Cape, 1936) was set in pre-Civil War Spain.

[17] Fedden was an artist whom Spender, Isherwood, and Heinz had known in Portugal.

[18] Lorca's "Romance de la Guardia Civil Espanola (a Juan Guerrero)" was collected in *Romancero Gitano*, poems written between 1924 and 1927.

[19] Hugo's *Spanish in Three Months*, part of a popular series of self-instruction books for various languages.

[20] Isherwood and Auden had begun work on their second play, *The Ascent of F6*, on March 16. According to *CaHK*, it was "written, revised, and typed out within one month" (p. 239).

[21] The following comments are appended in Spender's hand in ink.

[22] This letter to Auden was attached to the original of Letter 30. Because it is dated a few days later, it was probably posted to Auden separately, though it might have been an enclosure. Both letters are typewritten, with holograph notes appended.

[23] The GPO Film Unit, an information branch of the Post Office, was created in 1933. Auden worked with it for a time, collaborating with John Grierson (its director) and Benjamin Britten on *Night Mail*.

[24] Eliot's *Collected Poems: 1909–1935* (London: Faber and Faber, 1936) contained the first of the *Four Quartets*, "Burnt Norton."

[25] The following comments are appended in Spender's hand in ink.

[26] On February 4, Spender, his brother Humphrey, Isherwood, Heinz, and Tony visited a casino at Estoril. "Stephen, with bulging blue eyes and angry lobster cheeks, played at the highest table madly but carefully, and won nearly four hundred escudos" (*CaHK*, p. 233). During his visit, Isherwood and Heinz took Auden to Estoril, and out of that experience he wrote "Casino."

[27] *Forward from Liberalism*. Spender had published "Freud and Marx" in the *New Republic*, 86 (April 8, 1936), pp. 251-52. In addition, six poems (including three translations from Hölderlin) appeared over the next five years.

[28] The *TLS* reviewer wrote in "Symbols of Defeat" that in *The Burning Cactus* Spender "has by no means mastered the art of prose . . . but Mr. Spender's poetic originality is not absent from these pages. . . . He is handicapped by the fact that his themes are pathological rather than spiritual. These young men burst into tears on the slightest

provocation, dislike games, shudder at a woman's touch . . ." (April 18, 1936, p. 333).

[29] I. M. Parsons had written that Spender was "in a sense too involved in his material in *Vienna* to see it whole" (*Spectator*, 153, November 9, 1934, p. 728); William Troy in the *Nation*, 140 (March 13, 1935, p. 312) wrote that "the theme is there, and the emotions are there, but the two do not coalesce in a way that would give an ordered intensity to the whole."

[30] Auden had left for London on April 17 with the manuscript of *The Ascent of F6*.

[31] Collected in *The Still Centre* (London: Faber and Faber, 1939) under the title "Hölderlin's Old Age." In the published version, the final line reads "Burning vividly in the centre of a cold sky."

[32] If this poem was completed, it is unpublished.

[33] According to Christopher Isherwood (in conversation with the editor), Alfred was "a young French poet we knew in Portugal."

[34] Typewritten.

[35] Erwin Hansen went to Greece with Isherwood and Heinz. He is called Hans in Isherwood's *Down There on a Visit*.

[36] John Lehmann's magazine *New Writing* first appeared in the spring of 1936. According to its "Manifesto," it was "first and foremost interested in literature, and though it does not intend to open its pages to writers of reactionary or Fascist sentiments, it is independent of any political party."

[37] No poem appears on the reverse. If Spender included a poem on a separate sheet, it has been lost.

[38] Originally titled *Death of a Judge*, published by Faber and Faber as *Trial of a Judge* in March, 1938.

[39] Ramon J. Sender's *Seven Red Sundays* (London: Faber and Faber, 1936) describes an abortive proletarian revolt begun by the Anarchists, Communists, and Syndicalists during seven days in Madrid.

[40] Ralph Bates. See Part Three, note 16.

[41] "The Nowaks" (later collected in *Goodbye to Berlin*) appeared in the first issue of *New Writing*.

[42] Sir Moore Crosthwaite, who was educated at Oxford, entered the Diplomatic Service in 1932.

[43] Probably the Anglo-German Naval Agreement of June 18; it limited both British and German naval strength.

[44] Englebert Dollfuss, Austrian Prime Minister between 1932 and 1934. Leader of the Social Christian Party, Dollfuss was assassinated on July 25, 1934, in a Nazi raid on the Chancellery.

[45] The letter is typed; "If the Nazis . . .Viertel" is appended in Spender's hand, in ink.

[46] Aldous Huxley, *Eyeless in Gaza* (London: Chatto and Windus, 1934).

[47] In *Forward from Liberalism*, Spender writes "that prayers, the kind Huxley recommends, probably assisted Napoleon to take Moscow, Rockefeller to make his pile. . . . The human mind, like the human body, is capable of all sorts of obscenities" (p. 148). Of *Eyeless in Gaza* with its "constructive pacifist" hero, "I fear that, equipped with prayers, moral intuition, and a system of mental and physical exercises, the constructive pacifist possesses an apparatus which will enable him to withdraw from reality altogether" (p. 150). David Garnett, who reviewed *Eyeless in Gaza* for *The New Statesman and Nation*, June 20, 1936, failed "even to see that there is any connection between a writer's political and moral beliefs with his art" (p. 170). *The Daily Herald* "which represents the Labour Party in England conceals its opinions under the columns of the orthodox nonsense of the popular press, a fake nonconformist piety and photographs of royalty. In turning over its pages, the fingers of a few readers have been pricked by finding a socialist doctrine, the needle in this assorted haystack" (p. 114).

[48] Rosamond Lehmann, *The Weather in the Streets* (London: Collins, 1936). Jocelyn, a young writer who makes the narrator "sit quiet and consider ideas—that injustice matters and unemployment, and the power and hypocrisy of rulers, and revolutions, and Beethoven and Shakespeare and what poets think and write," is based on Spender.

[49] *Viewpoint*, "a revolutionary review of the arts," which was the publication of the British Section of the Writers' International, changed its name to *Left Review* in October, 1934. Chapter 13 of Spender's *The Destructive Element*, "Writers and Manifestos," had appeared there.

[50] Unidentified friend.

[51] According to Louis MacNeice's *The Strings are False*, Spender's

apartment had "a colour scheme out of *Vogue*, a huge vulcanite writing-desk and over the fireplace an abstract picture by Wyndham Lewis. Very comfortable and elegant but not quite big enough for Stephen; his enormous craggy apostolic flaring face seemed liable to burst its walls" (p. 166).

[52] Spender published three articles in *Left Review* in 1936: "An open letter to Aldous Huxley," "Fable and Reportage," and "Music and Decay" (a review of Joyce's *Ulysses*). Isherwood published nothing in the journal.

[53] Written on stationery imprinted with Spender's Queen's Mansions address.

[54] "Slightest effect on *writing*"; a single line is drawn through "writing," and "anything" is entered in Spender's hand.

[55] Typewritten to this point; what follows is appended in Spender's hand in ink.

[56] Spender did not travel to America until 1947.

[57] Autumn, 1936, issue of *Left Review*. In addition to *The Ascent of F6*, Spender also reviewed *New Writing* (II) and Auden's *Look, Stranger!* Of the *Ascent*, he wrote:

> Perhaps the best feature of the Auden-Isherwood dramatic style in *The Ascent of F6* is the rhythmic contrast which the writers maintain between two entirely different methods of presentation: firstly, realistic scenes of political reportage; secondly, fables. There are two approaches to the contemporary political scene: the one is direct, or partially satiric, external presentation; the other is fantasy or allegory.

[58] *The Ascent of F6*, directed by Rupert Doone, opened at the Mercury Theatre on February 26, 1937. See preface to Part Three.

[59] Lincoln Kirstein, a dance critic and novelist, was Director of the New York City Ballet. Auden dedicated his poem "Herman Melville" and his book *The Shield of Achilles* to Kirstein and his wife, Fidelma.

[60] Spender met Herbert List during his 1929 visit to Hamburg. See Letters 2 & 3.

[61] Written on stationery imprinted with Spender's Queen's Gardens address.

[62] "Who doesn't feel"—deleted.

[63] Mrs. Wallis Warfield Simpson, consort of King Edward VIII, was at this time the subject of a great deal of speculation. On December 9, Edward signed the Instrument of Abdication in order to remain with "the woman I love."

[64] Auden's "Letter to Lord Byron," written between July and October, 1936, was published in *Letters from Iceland* (with Louis MacNeice) by Random House in 1937.

[65] Written on stationery imprinted with the Queen's Mansions address.

[66] Giles Romilly, nephew of Winston Churchill, left Oxford to fight in Spain.

[67] That is, Tony's leaving to fight in Spain. See preface to Part Three.

[68] Written on stationery imprinted with the Queen's Mansions address.

[69] Written on Hotel de Bordeaux & d'Orient Marseilles stationery, with five single lines drawn through address.

[70] "I shall"—deleted.

[71] Spender's trip with Cuthbert Worsley to report on the sinking of the Russian ship *Comsomol*. See preface to Part Three.

[72] "Christopher"—deleted.

[73] "'Targeta Postal" postcard issued by the Comissariat de Propaganda de la Generalitat de Cataluña. Postmarked.

[74] In "A London Diary," Cyril Connolly charged that there "exists the typically English band of psychological revolutionaries, people who adopt left-wing political formulas because they hate their fathers or were unhappy at their public schools or insulted at the Customs or lectured about sex" (*The New Statesman and Nation*, January 16, 1937, pp. 73-4).

[75] Spender's poem "The Ambitious Son" appeared in the Christmas issue of *New Writing*, 1939.

Appendix:
The Line of the Branch—Two Thirties Journals

According to Kulkarni's *Spender Bibliography*, Stephen Spender kept two journals during the thirties, one in late 1932, another in late 1939. The text which follows was transcribed by the editor from the original notebooks, now housed in the Spender Archive at the Bancroft Library, University of California, Berkeley.

The 1932 journal, begun by Spender in Barcelona and previously unpublished, was kept in a ruled notebook. Twenty-three pages in holograph, it consists of a narrative of Spender and Hellmut's travels to Algeciras and Malaga in search of a house, as well as various "notes" on style, genius, and symbol. It concludes with drafts of two unpublished poems: "Oh love, forgive me" and "Possibility, possibility of a new life."

Spender started the 1939 journal on the day England declared war on Germany. He was depressed because Inez had left him, and he hadn't, as he told T. S. Eliot, "been able to work." "Yes," Eliot had replied, "that's an excellent idea. Just writing every day is a way of keeping the engine running, and then something good may come of it." Spender had been reading Gide's *Journals,* and his own journal parallels Gide's in its mixture of accounts of daily activities and literary gossip with passages of introspection and moral scrutiny. He published an excised version of this notebook as "September Journal" in the February, March, and May, 1940, issues of the newly established *Horizon* magazine; an even more heavily excised and rewritten version appeared in Spender's *The Thirties and After* (London: Macmillan, 1978). The original, kept like the 1932 journal in a ruled notebook, runs 104 pages in holograph.

1932 Journal

November 4, 1932. (Barcelona)

The woman with red lips sits on the bed. "We are all very Bohemian, here," she says, so we drink tea: two of us from proper cups, two from glasses, and our host who wears white flannels, four bracelets and a perpetual beret, from a cup without a handle. She talks to me about literature. She speaks of a woman novelist and remarks how she is approaching the period when women begin to get specially intelligent at the age of 55.

The German schoolmaster, who is a newcomer, begins to tell a story about the German Gesellschaft in Barcelona. He describes how all the ladies discuss their illnesses as sensationally as possible. One lady had colitis bacilli. I had told him in private that I had heard this illness could be infected in a certain manner, and now he wonders whether he dare tell our hostess this. "Oh please go on," she says, "we are all of us very Bohemian here." She asks H[ellmut] to sit in the bed beside her, he does so and lies down. She strokes his wrist. She says to me "So you are going to kidnap H. and take him away from us." She laughs. I laugh, but feel slightly irritated. H. looks up at me & smiles to show that he is not *in* this really & to wonder why it is that I can't be a little more amiable & forthcoming. I talk to our host who is nice in a very milky, narcissistic kind of way.

Then the lady starts talking her native Czech. She encourages H. to say the one sentence which he knows in Czech. He does so, she hides her face in the sheets & heaves with laughter. The schoolmaster is very amused and he talks Polish. They giggle again. Our host says "Stephen is shocked." H. looks very nicely at me, but he is perhaps disappointed: I don't know. I am not in this at all. I feel as out of it as I do when people start community singing. It is just the same feeling as I had at school when the football team was cheered. I do not even attempt to look pleased; in fact, I attempt to look shocked. Without much interest I wonder whether H. will be able to put up with my behaving like this. People who are intoxicated by company find it very difficult to forgive one for not joining in their games.

Nov. 5.

His mother writes that she was happy between the ages of 17 & 23.
He himself having starved in the streets of Berlin
And being at the mercy of devouring Kindness
From Jews, knows happiness now only as a fever
Sometimes recurring from another life. At the age of 22
Being of our generation, the memories which he hoards
Are all from childhood. His possessions he hangs on to.
Politics he hates. He does not look forward.
He hopes that perhaps another tidal wave
Like Noah's, will drown Europe.

Nov. 7th.

The central regret for the person who does not care for money & who belongs to our class or who can afford not to care, is that yet he is dependent on money for his self expression. For this reason he would willingly destroy himself economically in order to overthrow the whole system. The central regret for the person who is intellectual & who realizes that intellectualism has no absolute moral worth is that he is dependent for this realization on his intellect. Therefore he wishes to prostrate himself to a class of people who are unintellectual. Therefore he hates other intellectual people with whom he has most in common. Yet he is not understood by the people with whom he has nothing in common & his appeal, being from the intellect, does not reach them.

The only reason why I should ever be jealous of H. is the fear that he should go away from me. This is not fair because ultimately I hold myself absolutely free from him. For instance, if I wanted to go and live in a slum I doubt if he would do so too, but I should go there just the same.

Nov. 17th.

I got up at half past six & fetched H. from the Hotel Bristol. We took a taxi to our boat arriving at 7:30 only to find that it was not due to go till 11. So we walked about Barcelona for 3½ hours, had coffee, etc.

We went on board again at 11 o'clock and, after a further two hours of waiting the cargo boat, the *Capa Tres Forcas*, left the harbour. The morning lovely & the sea quite smooth. Very blue as if coloured. After we had left Barcelona we kept close to the coast which is mountainous, till almost 3 p.m. when we went further out to sea. The mountains from the sea looked modeled as if out of clay. A beautiful gray-moss colour, the highlights of gold. All day we have been going South, or South-West, straight into the sun. We sit in the stern & the shadows always fall towards us, whilst the tackle with the sun on it and the bow gleam in our eyes. Hellmut very happy. I also felt very happy but I spent a lot of the afternoon feeling remorse for my laziness. I felt slightly ill for about ½ an hour after we had left Barcelona, but now am quite all right.

Nov. 18th.

We slept well in our cabin & there were no fleas. We woke at six to see the ship moving against the lighthouse on the mole of Valencia harbour. We got up a little later and watched the sun rising whilst we were tugged by the iron hawsers pulled by donkey engines against the quay. The landing took almost half an hour. As soon as we could do so we left the boat and walked along a very long road through the harbour quarter into Valencia and then we drank coffee & ate rolls. We explored the town, and saw the cathedral. Baroque angels: devout but worldly gestures: their tears, perfect rainbow-coloured spheres. Also some sort of a baroque palace fronted with slabs of different-coloured marble, and with round the door a huge oozing marble ornament of gods & goddesses; melting rich like wax. A church with spiralling aspiring sugar-candy pillars. Apart from these four or five buildings, Valencia seems to be a monstrous and extravagantly built Southern town with any number of towers and angels and buildings that look as if they were done after a model made by a child with a box of coloured bricks.

At 4.00 p.m. we returned to the boat, which they were still loading, and which, as usual, did not sail till four hours after the time of departure. The shadows now long, the light on the moving figures of the workmen, seeming highly glazed and cinematographic. We loaded oranges, bales of tobacco, empty barrels of wine. As we had so much time Hellmut & I walked to the further end of the quay and watched some poor people fishing. They all seemed very inexpert, and missed bites, and threw their lines muddled into the water; but at last someone caught a bass of almost 2 lbs. weight. We were all very excited. Hellmut was fascinated by the appearance of one of the fishermen: an old man with long thick dirty ebony hair and beard, parchment but frank face and deep-set black eyes. He wore corduroy trousers which were old and highly polished about the knees. Again a very happy day.

At night the mast and rigging of the ship were like a tree hung with stars.

The men who represented the firms which had loaded their goods in the ship sat in the saloon with money bags in front of them, and bargained like people in the Old Testament.

Nov. 19.

We got up at 7 o'clock, as the ship was drawing into Alecante. Then we walked along the quay and along the boulevard of the harbour and had breakfast in the outdoor restaurant of a hotel. After breakfast we walked further along the boulevard till we reached the fish market. In front of the quay fishing boats were unloading baskets of sardines. In the market itself there were open boxes of sardines, ink fish, shellfish, and fish of rainbow colours, all wet and glittering. Near the boxes were lying two huge tunny fish which look as if their skin is made of black leather; they have [jagged] saw fins, their mouths are like iron, and the flesh is red like raw beef. It took two men to carry one of these tunny fish. Then we went through the town and up a hill which had a stone road built zigzagging across it, and along one side of which is built the old city wall. On the top of the hill, surrounded by a forking of the wall is the castle. Little foliage on the hill, the colour of rocks & lava gray-gold, the cactuses prussian blue, the new walls which bank up the road a bright pale orange. The castle itself lay flat and monotonous on the table-top of the hill with its lines simply broken but predominantly horizontal like the shape of a dreadnought. The sky lightly clouded and magenta, the sea a light sapphire colour, and seen at a different level in a bay beyond a point of land. The grounds and interior of the castle were very beautiful. H. was very excited and disappointed because we had not enough film to take pictures of everything. We came down from the hill & went through a part of the town with little houses built against the side of the hill. It was now 11 o'clock and all the inhabitants of these houses, men, women, lots of children, as many cats, rather fewer dogs, cocks, hens, a turkey, had left their houses and transferred the whole history of their lives out of doors. The scene was laid out in front of us with all the variety of everyday life rather like one of those wall pictures in which the artist has depicted every kind of object and activity in order that children may learn in a foreign language as many different names as possible. Above the houses on the hillside washing was spread out. In the foreground just below us children explored an enormous rubbish heap for treasures. The children wore only a smock down to the waist and were very dirty. Hellmut was very excited by this scene and also by Alecante. We then went back into the town & sat down & drank coffee. After lunch we went into the cathedral, which did not interest us, and then we watched children playing football in the square in front of another very ornamental building. It started to rain now so we had to have some more coffee and we talked (mostly about sex) until it was time for the ship to sail.

Nov. 20.
There was a storm and I was sick almost the whole day. Nov. 21st arrived Malaga. 22 & 23 in Malaga.

Nov. 26.
On the morning of the 23d we left Malaga & started to walk along the coast in the direction of Gibraltar in order that we might look for a house to live in. The first twelve kilometers were dull, but then the mountains stretched near to the sea & the landscape was very beautiful. We had lunch in a resort called Torremolinos, which was very attractive. The weather was beautiful, the sea a very dark blue flushed with white, for the wind was still rather strong. We found an insect which I think is called the praying mantis (it is certainly described in Fabre) and we amused ourselves with this a long time making it pray and seeing it in its fighting attitude with its wings spread out. H. was very happy the whole day & said that we would walk right to Gibraltar. At night we slept in a village called Fuengirola; the Fonda was good & clean. Before Fuengirola we passed through a very beautiful village called San Candidia.

On the 24th we walked along a less interesting part of the coast. The mountains were now retreating inland and the country by the west was mostly dunes covered with a thick palm-shrub. H. was rather depressed all the morning & very tired. After almost 9 k. walk we made a pause at a little inn, as a lorry was waiting outside it, and we thought we might persuade the driver to take us to Marbella. We had a very nasty kind of lemonade in this inn & we hung about a long time whilst the driver and two other men who accompanied him had their lunch, but H. did not dare to speak to the men, so finally we went further on our way. Thursday was altogether a bad day as there was no village between Fuengirola and Marbella, and we had not been able to buy anything for lunch in Fuengirola except bread, condensed milk, stale chocolate & some very [dry] oranges. We ate these things on the beach & then went further. H. was very tired but he cheered up considerably. We came to a more attractive part of the west where the road led through pine woods, sweet smelling, mild and hygienic like the country near a health resort. Then we left the pine woods & we came again to hills. Beyond a ridge we could make out Marbella, inland were the mountains, and beyond Marbella, stretching to the South West, were the point of Gibraltar & a further point beyond that not connected to the land, which we took to be the coast of Africa. But it may have been the Punta Mauroqui, and yet a further disconnected point of land to the South may have been Africa. As we descended towards the village the sun was setting, and its reflection lay in the sparkling and azure sea like a path of hammered [metal]. The crests of the far-off rocks floated on evening vapours which looked like yellow pollen.

We rested a little until the sun had set, as H. was so footsore he could only walk with difficulty, and besides this, he was having pain. By the time we had reached the village it was almost dark. A small boy said he would show us the way to the Fonda, & he led us through what seemed a great many winding and narrow lanes between houses to a square. Just before we reached the square, whilst we were in one of the lanes, H. told me not to look round, as some children were following us, and a moment later a stone struck me. We went into the square which, in the half-dark, we saw was filled with children, all of whom stared at us, and many of whom followed us as we walked round the square looking for a Fonda. There seemed to be no people older than some mature but idiotically childish-looking girls. Then we saw a carbinero and he shouted to the children to leave us alone, but they took no notice. The children screamed at us, but they did not seem at all gay and they all seemed very ugly. We found the Fonda but we did not like it, so then, always followed by children, we walked down one of the side lanes & we asked a wrinkled old lady if there were another Fonda. She said yes, at the opposite side of the square. We returned to the square, and walked through the crowd of children again to the other Fonda, which we did not see at once, but when we found it, it was even nastier than the first one. So we returned to the first Fonda & some of the bolder of the children came running into it after us, like some pest which we could not shake off. Hellmut was in great pain & we sat in the hall & he was unable to move. Then he bargained with the landlady & she showed us our room. We sat on our bed very relieved to be alone and then we laughed because H. almost at once found a flea which had settled on the back of his hand. After almost an hour we were able to have supper, but there was practically nothing which H. could eat. I ate fish & meat which were perfectly good, but very unappetizingly served, the fish, for example being cooked complete with head, eyes, fins, scaly skin, and tail, and in no way "dressed," but just fried complete in oil. Before supper H. had gone out again to get some medicine & he took doses before & after supper & so was better. I was very upset at seeing him so ill. Seeing that I was upset, he pulled himself together a lot. Then we talked & agreed that we would not walk any further.

The next morning we got up at about 8.30 and went to a café by the shore to have breakfast. There were not so many children in the streets now, but we were very much stared at & we noticed that a number of the people had the appearance of idiots. At the café we had our shoes cleaned by a stupid looking shoe-cleaner who took at least ten minutes very languidly to polish each shoe. In the road in front of the café there were a number of mongrels and a dog which seemed to be the principal whore-bitch of the district. This dog had been fucked lame so that it could hardly walk, and also apparently blind, by the other dogs, and whilst we were having coffee we watched it have intercourse made incomplete because it could not stand with at least four other dogs. During the rest of the day when we were in Marbella whenever we passed down that road, the dog was being used. The sex-life of these dogs seemed typical of life in Marbella, judging from the number of children & idiots in the place. We watched some older children playing but they seemed to play like idiots without joy. Indeed the whole place seemed singularly joyless, and Hellmut said one had the feeling that it was a collection of people who had somehow lost their happiness and who could only breed. The town itself was quite pretty with an attractive church & with a white square with palm trees in it. At night, as we walked through the narrow lanes of whitewashed houses, above the dark path of the sky with large frosty stars was singularly beautiful. But we both hated the place & were upset.

At half past three we left in an autobus for La Linea. We passed through an attractive looking fishing town called Estepona. On our way between Marbella & Estepona I noticed that some children had laid a path of sharp flints across the road in order to puncture the tires of motorcars. In Estepona a boy of the size of a child of about eight years old came to the door of the omnibus & tried to sell me some lottery tickets. He was a hunchback & had an old, toothless mouth, & the face of a lecherous old man. There was also an idiot beggar who came up to us to beg & then he went away from the car a few paces to a restaurant where he tried to sit down. An official of the omnibus & postal service gave him a severe blow on the back of the head with a stick. The idiot grinned & sat down in the chair & waved gaily to us as the omnibus moved off. The official with the stick seemed almost as complete an idiot, but a more murderous one, as the man he had hurt.

When we arrived at La Linea we were welcomed by crowds of porters, taxi drivers, boys, etc., all talking English. We avoided them & started to walk to another square where we might get a taxi. As we were going along the road, I noticed a policeman in a side street rescuing a dog from some children who had tied a cord round its neck and were apparently trying to hang it. In Alecante we stopped some children stoning a cat. The children seem often to be a fit subject for Thomas Hardy in their abnormal cruelty. We got a taxi which took us towards Gibraltar, but first of all we were held up at the Customs. I held out my Pass & said "I am an Englishman." Hellmut was very amused because the policeman said "Rightho, we are all Englishmen here." Then we had to get out and were asked innumerable stupid questions which had the effect of alarming H. disproportionately, so that he was white & shivering. We were given leave to stay a night in the Hotel Victoria where the taxi then took us.

As soon as we arrived in the hotel and had a decent room given to us, H. was delighted and happy, and almost at once we went out and walked down the main street. By night the main street of Gibraltar is very comic & belongs to the world of expensively made tone films. Ordinary English policemen, naval police, & military police, walk about the place, looking after the civil, naval, and military population; Arabs, Egyptian Jews and dagos of every kind, fantastically dressed in bathtowels, dressing gowns, red fezes, and with sensuous, virile black eyes and moustaches, give a spirit of evil to the street, in which English towns are usually lacking; the bookshops are almost frantically crammed with goody goody literature for the officers' children as an antidote I suppose to the exotic spicing; there are peg-toothed soldiers, bull-dog-breed sailors (who were a great disappointment to H.), army, naval & civil chaplains, lots of men with big, purple-veined noses & well-whiskied voices, polo-players, eager tipsters, pimps and touts. Hellmut was very happy, and rather worried because I did not find myself sufficiently at home: he is always getting shocked by my lack of "stimmung" doing things which make him enthusiastic. We had supper & then we went into a café, and a tout came up to me and said he was sure he had seen me in Battersea, but finally we agreed it must have been my double. The sailors were very affectionate with each other & lived up to their reputations by dancing [together]. But at 11 o'clock the lights of the restaurants & cafés were put out & we were all sent to bed.

Nov. 26. [later]

This morning we talked about money, had baths, & I wrote my diary. We met Sir Heskett Bell in the main street and accompanied him to Algeciras.

I felt remorse about work all the afternoon and the desire to settle down.

Nov. 28. (Algeciras)

There are two Americans in this hotel, a mother, a woman of about 55, and her son, aged about thirty. They both wear, or give the impression of wearing, the same kind of square hornrimmed spectacles, and they are always cold in this hotel, which is certainly not too warm. In the evening they both come down to dinner in greatcoats. They live in Connecticut and they keep a dog. The son so obviously wanted to talk to someone that finally we did talk to him. He talked in a slow, ugly, but good-natured drawl about his fifteen months in Europe. A bad cold in Switzerland, measles in Italy, followed by whooping cough as soon as he had recovered; now, in Spain, apparently once more a bad cold. He told us the hotel in Cadiz was very good & cheap, we then reckoned how many cents there were to a £, and we discussed the possibility of a return of the monarchy in Germany. Hellmut was so bored that he went to bed. This talk had on me the effect of a waking dream in which through a haze of some occurrence which is actually happening, one cannot prevent oneself thinking of other things which belong entirely to a world of fantasy. After Hellmut had gone to bed the mother joined me & her son, bringing with her the dog. They told me that they had not been able to visit England, and at the present moment they were obliged to be in Algeciras instead of Gibraltar, on account of this animal. I suppose that in Gibraltar the dog would be suspected by the English of espionage. The Americans are leaving Gibraltar by the Italian boat on Tuesday; but a policeman must take them through the town with their dog. A few days ago they were in Cadiz and they had taken berths on a Spanish ship to New York. At the booking office they inquired carefully whether their dog would be allowed in the cabin with the mother. The answer was yes, certainly. In order to make doubly sure, on the day before the boat sailed the mother went aboard the ship, and seeing a man there she asked if she might speak to the captain. "I am the captain," said the man. "Well then," asked the mother "May I take my dog in the cabin with me tomorrow?" "Yes certainly," he said. The next day they went on board early, and after a time, this same man knocked at the door of the cabin, and said that the dog must be put in the hold. "But you said yesterday that we might have him with us," said the mother. "Well, the captain says he must go in the hold." "Why but aren't you the captain?" "No, I'm not," said the man. On hearing this the mother, son, & dog with only their hand luggage, left the ship ten minutes before it sailed. Their trunks are still on it, now in America, but they hope to have their passages refunded.

November 29 (Malaga)

We returned by the bus to Malaga. The afternoon was lovely but very windy with clouds coming up against the wind, and rather cold. The shadows of the clouds were like huge clearly defined ink blots on the glazed magenta mountains. We sat, as before, in the 3rd class part of the bus. For part of the way a short, fat, dark, lively, unshaved man sat next to me, who jumped about a lot and who spat in a careful circle all round his feet. Hellmut had much worse luck. Next to him was a youth of about twenty who looked like an overgrown child of twelve. He was fair with short cut hair and he wore spectacles with lenses round like magnifying glasses, but chipped & dirty. He spat industriously but not so expertly as the man at my side, in imitation of him. He had an enormous and festering boil on the side of his face nearest to me, and a big scar above the bridge of his nose. He talked in a squeaky voice very rapidly. When I sit next to people of this sort in public vehicles, I indignantly detest them, and I wish that I were some kind of a feudal tyrant who could order them to be killed. They seem an insult to humanity, a contradiction to the assertive feeling that human life is beautiful, generous & worth living. I thought how very different the German proletarians are from these people. A Berlin workman would not have failed to show his disgust with my companions in the bus.

When we got to Malaga we fetched our post & took it to the hotel. I had letters to say that Isaiah Berlin[1]* was ill, Marg Paine dead, Michael [Spender]'s friend Erika ill, and Granny worried. Hellmut was reading a letter from his mother & he said "einmal täglich, Stephen, einmal täglich," as I understood him. I said "What, opium do you mean?" and he explained that he had meant ein mark. His mother, apart from the rent which he sends her, now has 6 mrk a week to live on, 1 mrk each weekday for food and a card for fish on Sundays. H. explained this to me and then he burst into tears & wept & wept. I sat on my bed thinking how good he was, and how terrible it all was, with my brain, but yet it all seemed to have no meaning, and really I was hoping that he would cheer up & entertain me soon, and I was wondering when I would be able to get my supper, and if I ought to take his hand or stroke his hair to comfort him, or would this only disgust him? When he was better, I went out to buy some cigarettes, and then when I came back he was all right, and he kissed me & when we went to supper he was gay and perfectly normal in his behavior. He has tenderness in his nature. When he most needs comforting it is always he who comforts me.

Hellmut's Dreams. Hellmut dreamt last night that for five minutes he had forgotten all the cares of the past, and was only aware of facts & of his existence. The colour of forgetfulness was yellow of a certain shade & also it had a round shape & a size which he could not explain to me.

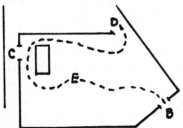

He dreamt there was a race between the Graf Zeppelin & racing cars the shape of torpedoes. The cars also somehow represented forgetfulness.

He dreamt he was in a room (which he drew & which I have copied out) and he was asleep in a chaise longue. Sleeping beside him was Frau Eckner. Eckner came into the room by

---

*Notes to the Appendix begin on p. 207.

door B and he advanced into the room as far as the point E. Then Hellmut was aware of his looking at them & of the feeling of jealousy: He then walked out of the room round the chaise longue, not out of the nearest door, C, but out of the door D. After this, there was some sort of trouble on account of a garter belonging to Frau Eckner. Now this garter was the same as a pair which Hellmut had seen some boys wearing in Alecante. He thought of saying to me how he liked the boys' stockings & garters and bare knees and then he had a slight feeling that I might possibly be troubled or jealous if he said this, and it was better to leave things alone, so he said nothing.

Last night he also dreamt that he was in a girl's dress which reached to the end of his penis, just covering it, so that he was anxious all the time lest he might be exposed. In his desire to wear girls' clothes he is always troubled by the problem of what to do with his hair and now he noticed a boy wearing a red bandage which bound his head so that the hair showed just under the bandage. The bandage suggested the colour of blood, but it was not quite that colour. When we were in Algeciras Hellmut had noticed a boy with fair hair wearing a bandage & he thought how pretty this covering was. But the bandage was a saffron colour, though the fact of its being a bandage of course suggested the idea of blood. In his dream not only was the bandage red, but the hair it covered was not the boy's, but Hellmut's own.

Hellmut can draw what he sees in his dreams. He is very exhausted by telling me about them, but he seems to desire to tell them. In fact this morning he told me a lot of this whilst he was still in a half sleep.

Nov. 30.

Today & yesterday have been two very domestic days. Yesterday we spent most of the afternoon at home in our room in the hotel reading or working. In the morning two young Englishmen were here who remembered me from Oxford. A car, one fur-lined and one [brocaded] greatcoat, drinks all the way across country, a house in Tangier to which we were invited, literary friends. One of the young men [has] a moustache, paints & easel, a chauffeur who "knows all the cut-throats in Spain & Algiers." Tales of how they blackmail people, some complicated arrangement by which they were travelling with a lady's maid who sat in front of the car with a chauffeur. They will return [home] in 8 days by air from Algeciras. They were friendly & talked with that accent which is at once superior, and at the same time grimaces and cuts on the speaker's lips like a flunkey before one.

Hellmut was very much disgusted & seriously afraid I might go to Tangier. We had supper at home then coffee in a restaurant, where Hellmut told me about his dreams. We were very affectionate all of yesterday. Yet H. questioned me again, because he is always anxious to prove that I am fond of him, but that my fondness is unlike that of the hundreds of people who have been physically attracted by him.

Today. We looked again for rooms or a house, but as usual with no success. Beautiful colours of a donkey laden with fruits and green vegetables which we passed. Also the splendid thick piled-on colours of fruit & vegetables in the markets. Lettuce, tomatoes, oranges, pepper-fruit, custard-apples, pomegranates; bananas, lemons, tangerines with their leaves, grapes, radishes, young celery, nuts, all together, pell-mell, in profusion. Hellmut had some pain again. We bought a spirit lamp, alcohol, three spoons, an earthenware jar & our supper & ate at home. We are very low in money & Hellmut does everything he can to save. I hate saving and am always trying to buy useless additional things just in order to spend a little extra money. I would often prefer something expensive & bad to something cheap & good. But H. understands this & restrains me. He went home with the shopping, leaving me to get some eggs which took some time to find as [dairies] are rare. When I came back to our room the lights were out & H. was seated in his bed while on the table between our beds he had spread the supper & set two candles burning, and there our little spirit lamp was burning also. The candles threw a warm and soft light on the grapes & bread. We had supper by candlelight, sitting on our beds. We boiled some eggs & also made tea with the stove. The egg shells, grape skins, crumbs, an empty tin for jam, and the old tea leaves we wrapped into a big parcel, and then having put out the light in our room, we threw the parcel into the [enclosed] garden opposite our window on the other side of the road, where the hens must thrive on our waste.

Notes.

Style. Perfection of style would be a language which everyone could understand with absolute clarity and equal intuition. What we call style in a great writer is the blunders which his humanity compels him to make in his endeavours to obtain to the perfect means of expression. But these blunders are his personality & his humanity & therefore what, as human beings, we are able to understand him by.

He makes a synthesis out of his incompleteness in the same way as Beethoven was able to use as material for his music the discordant noises which he heard in his ears instead of hearing.

Genius. Wyndham Lewis's conception of genius as the ego in solitude [contemptuously] hating the rest of [humanity] is surely nonsense. Genius is humanity & genius is irresistably comprehensible to human beings, however much they hate having to recognize it. The man of genius is the man who is able to express the universality of the human spirit. . . . He is like the volcano out of which pours the lava which is also beneath all the crust of the earth surrounding the volcano. What most people call genius is virtuosity: virtuosity is specialization in some particular activity or branch of knowledge, and it is in no sense universal.

These observations clumsy: observations of a boy of 16.

Dec. 6.

We failed completely to find a house, so we are on the *Cabo Huertas* going back to Barcelona. I partly hope that we may in some way be detained at Alecante as I have a strong feeling against Barcelona. Hellmut has been having a bad cold & still is not well.

A few days ago we walked up the hill to see the ruins of the castle & old wall just outside Malaga. We took a wrong turning and got into one of those streets where all the children run after one, shouting "penny! penny!" We finally got half way up the hill & then it started to rain and we ran down along a stony path, through the quarter inhabited by poor people with these children. A feeling as though one is in dark room with a bat always flying into one's face.

I had a headache during the last two days. Was absorbed in an unreal world from which I could not shake myself. The necessity of doing things, and the reality of objects & people outside this world irritating. A feeling as if the veins of a leaf were growing in my head.

In the barber's shop. Lather. My mouth a red wound swathed in a white bandage. In Spain the barbers carry on telephone conversations, conversations with people in the street, they spit on the floor, they leave the shop whilst they go to look at a woman in the street, they smoke cigarettes, all whilst they are in the middle of shaving you. There is always a very small boy in these shops who brushes one's clothes as one goes out, and who can never reach higher than my waist with his brush.

Hellmut and I both so sensitive that we can't argue with each other at all. Hellmut argues like a woman. He always makes the argument personal, and he goes further than this because he takes one's words &twists them round so that one has said something very *méchant* to him.

I think that he explains people, he does not understand them.

He explains about himself. There is always something important which he will not tell. He has a real passion for the truth & suffers because there is always something which he cannot tell the truth about. He tries to make up for this by rather exaggerating the importance of revelations which he can make.

I have the stupidity & the intelligence, the openness & the tiresome subtlety of an educated savage. Irritating to be with me.

The building of the ship, bridge, poop, etc., like flat, gay, painted cardboard scenery moving with its snowy wash through the very dark blue sea.

Last night before we left Malaga we had coffee & played patience after our evening meal. We were very happy & gay. Now we rag each other a lot & have invented a language of crude insults which we play when we are in good humours, which we usually are, in spite of illness & poetry etc. (This game tends to become rough & excites me a little sexually; also H. I think.) After we had finished our coffee & our game we went to a cake shop to buy a few cakes. In this shop I nearly trod on an almost fully grown, pretty black & white puppy which yelped. Then we saw that this puppy had only three legs. The other leg was cut off at the paw & was bloody & disgusting. Hellmut gave an exclamation of disgust & hid his face in his hand & said, "These people are horrible, how can they be so cruel." He was very depressed & we did not buy enough cakes (though I went back & got some afterwards), and we walked down the road to the harbour, discussing the cruelty of the Spaniards which besides maiming them, allows maimed animals to live, & does not look after children properly so that they become blind or crippled by carelessness. H. was terribly upset; he gave the impression, as he sometimes does, that he had lost his balance completely & did not even want to regain it. We went to the harbour to see a rather swell, white, expensively lit pleasure steamer which was at the quay next to the *Cabo Huertas* (our boat), and I tried to distract H.'s attention because another three legged dog was at the quayside amongst a crowd of people. But he saw it. We talked till very late about plans for the future.

Now at night the surf which the ship, as she steams before a strong following breeze, throws forward, is like a field of snow, slowly expanding & then retreating. The shadow of the ship's bow & anchor cast on the surf is like the shadow of a building which a light casts on a snowy street.

December 9.

Two days ago, we were again in Alecante. We walked up the hill to the castle again in order that I might take some photos. The castle is built on an huge overhanging rock above which its low walls jut. It looks as if the rock, which rests on a very steep hill and which has huge fissures in it, might any day fall and destroy the old part of Alecante, directly below it. The castle is not very high, but directly one has entered its stone gate the courtyard seems as high as [an] eagle, and near the sun. Through the gates and above the walls one sees the hills washed in the pale colours of Southern anemones. One approaches the castle from the back. When one comes to the front which looks down on Alecante, one can hear the noise of the city below, mostly a rattling, and occasionally a single voice becomes very distinct, or a dog barking or a hooter. Yesterday we were in Valencia.

Today we arrived at Tarragona. I woke up with my cold much worse, and I keep on sneezing, and I feel as if my head were being held under a shower of slimy water. The day was lovely, and at 10.30 a.m. the boat drew in to Tarragona which is on a hill. It is really more beautiful than any place we have seen yet. In Tarragona there is a small zoo, mostly for birds and monkeys, which we visited this morning. It is most curiously arranged. In one cage were collected a goat, a goose, a peacock and a deer. In another were two peacocks, male & female, and a sheep, tied to a strong chain. In a third was a parrot, some gardening tools and a keeper's uniform. It is the sort of zoo George III might have [delighted in] when he was [mad].

This afternoon Hellmut went on by train to Barcelona, in order to fix up about our rooms, if it is possible. I feel rather lonely without him. Also I dread the society at Barcelona, and I wish I had protested more strongly against returning there. However I expect my cold makes me feel this.

Symbols for the heat of the sun. (1.) The feeling of the warm deck of a sailing boat, bright, rough, warm-smelling, light planks. (2) The sense of hammering & light outside as though they were laying a carpet for a bride. (3) A courtyard, one side in a shadow, silence. (4)

The inside of a tent, the cloth made transparent & vivid chrome yellow. (5) The inside of a barn, one beam with motes floating in it, murmuring afternoon outside. (6) A street, a dock, many labourers noisily working, all washed in strong white light, above the noise of working a feeling that a huge silence of white light is flooding over them, and that this stretches for hundreds of miles all round them, as far as Venice.

Dec. 14.

Yesterday we moved into our apartment here. It is v[ery] nice. A large light living room, a bedroom, a kitchen & a bathroom. The gas & electricity do not function yet, so yesterday we had supper by candlelight. We are very short for cash and I had to cash a cheque through Arthur Loveday to pay the rent. I think I must be about £50 overdrawn now. Uncle Loveday was rather sceptical about our arrangements, he refused to believe that we could not find a house near Malaga & he also refused to meet Hellmut on the ground that he hated all Germans. I took revenge by asking the maid whether Herr Loveday was at home very loudly yesterday when I went to lunch there. He is a nice man but his being such an ardent Christian plus his distrust of people who have not been to public schools, plus his love of people who can play polo, all make things very difficult.

We went to the market yesterday and bought stores of food for our meals. Now that we have these rooms we both have a great desire to buy things, which we have to repress firmly. The shops are very nice now in the evenings when they are lit or gaily decorated for Xmas.

> Oh love, forgive me for the ideal without scruple
> Which feeds on denial, an angel & destroyer
> Of a beauty at once serene and horrible—
> Accept me at last as your pupil.

Irritating to see someone well wrapped up & taking care of himself. A bad sign: someone who looks like an angel when he has an orgasm.

> Possibility, possibility of a new life:
> Forget at last those claims & chains
> In which we grew. The house with the open door
> Regards the hammer-headed cloud. At evening the rocks,
> Rusted like crests of pistil, rest upon

The waves of yellow pollen. Let our delights
Forever twine their dazzling necks like birds,
And make no close demand, offence
Destroying the vulnerable free balance
Of equal love.

1939 Journal

I am going to keep a journal because I cannot accept the fact that I feel so shattered that I cannot write at all. Today I read in the papers a story by Seymour Hicks of a request he gave to Wilde after his imprisonment, to write a play. Wilde said: "I *will* write a wonderful play with wonderful dialogue." As he said this Hicks realized that he would never write again.

I feel as if I could not write again. Words seem to break in my mind like sticks when I put them down on paper. I cannot see how to spell some of them. Sentences are covered with leaves, and I really cannot see the line of the branch that carries the green meaning.

It so happens that the world has broken just at the moment when my own life has broken. . . .

I know that she cannot bear being with me when my forehead is split with anxiety. I drive a wedge through her on those occasions and she makes me feel that I am being cruel to her and almost treating her violently. When Toller[2] died she threw the brooch which *he* had given her at my feet and said, "You know people with violent passions who are capable of hanging themselves." I am glad I am not imposing my presence on her now.

The best thing is to write anything, anything at all that comes into your head, until gradually there is a calm and creative day. It is absolutely essential to be patient and to remember that nothing one feels is the last word; all feeling passes over me and as far as the life of the emotions goes there is only one rule: to wait. . . .

The most dangerous deception the emotions can practice on you is to pretend to be timeless and absolute. On top of despair, they impose a boredom which tells you that nothing is or ever will be worth doing, that all the words have broken into the separate letters of the alphabet & cannot be put together again. The whole of your life, they say, will be like this. Your unhappiness is no longer just a sensation; it is a plant growing through your whole body and separating the brain. Not only is it going to be impossible for your mind ever to do anything but just stare, without crystalizing your disparate sensations, but today too is expanding into an infinity of boredom. It is now ten o'clock and one o'clock will not come: or not until a whole sea of empty aging has flooded your mind.

That is how Wilde must have felt sitting with his two boys at his marble topped table. That is how hundreds of people waiting for the news bulletins on the wireless feel today. But there is another waiting which is not just the emptiness of waiting. This is the patient faith of waiting. Realizing that everything is only an episode in a whole story and although one has not control of the episode one can gradually form the whole pattern, however terrible the setbacks of moments or even of years.

I must put out my hands and grasp the handful of facts. How extraordinary they are! The aluminium balloons seem nailed into the sky like those bolts which hold together the radiating struts of a biplane between the wings. The streets become more and more deserted, and the West End is full of shops to let. Sandbags are laid above the glass pavements over basements along the sidewalk. Last night during the blackout there was a tremendous thunderstorm. We stood at the bottom of Regent Street in the pouring rain, the pitch darkness broken intermittently by tremendous flashes of sheet lightning which lit up everything like broad daylight. Today Tony and I had lunch with Cyril and Jeannie.[3] She had been trying to get a taxi last night in the same blackout. After a great deal of waiting one stopped. The taxi[driver] said, "I'm free ma'am, but perhaps I'd better not take you because I've just been set on by two men," and he held up his handkerchief which was completely soaked in blood. She said, "No, perhaps you'd better take care of yourself." He drove away into the darkness.

Yesterday afternoon I was standing at the bottom of Archer Street outside the P.O. when a little dappled pony attached to a milk cart seemed to go completely off its head. It whimpered, kicked the front of the cart violently with its hind legs, trying to break all the bottles, and occasionally it started swinging round, forcing the cart against the curb. The milkman was in a telephone box, phoning presumably for assistance. People stood round staring neither with amusement nor annoyance, but a kind of faint sympathy as though the pony was expressing just what they were feeling.

September 4

The king broadcast a speech last night which was badly spoken enough, I should have thought, to finish the Royal Family in this country. It was a great mistake. He should never be allowed to say more than twenty words. After this his voice has the effect of a very spasmodic and often interrupted tape machine. It produces an effect of colourless monotony, except that after a very slow and drawn out passage sometimes the words are all jumbled together at the end of a sentence. First of all one tries to listen to what he is saying. Then one forgets this and starts sympathizing with him in his difficulties. Then one wants to smash the radio. Later there were Greenwood & Sinclair.[4] They talked about gallant Poland, our liberties, democracy, etc., in a way which raised very grave doubts in my mind. Greenwood even talked about fighting the last war to end war. Personally, I prefer Chamberlain's line to all this sanctimoniousness, which is that he has done his best to give Hitler everything but feels that now he can give nothing more. I dislike all the talk about God defending the right. God has always defended the right, and after such a long experience, he of all people must have realized the utter futility of it. Personally, if I were a close advisor of God, I'd press him to decide the issue one way or the other once and for all, and not go on playing this cat and mouse game between right and wrong.

The whole point of being a man is that there is no omnipotence on one's side. One doesn't have to choose between good and evil, right and wrong, but between various kinds of evil. It is not a conflict between God & the Devil, Christ & Judas, but between the systems represented by Chamberlain and Hitler respectively.

With all humility, I am on the side of the Chamberlain system against fascism. The fundamental personal reason is that I hate the idea of being regimented and losing my own freedom of action. I carry this feeling too far; in fact, I must admit, leaving it to the power of hysteria, I dread being ordered about and made to do what I don't want to do. This fear has even forced me into a kind of isolation, in which I find that the personalities of my fellow beings often impose a kind of restraint and sense of obligation on me.

There you are; you analyse your hatred of fascism and it comes to a desire to be left alone. At school you allowed the other boys to take everything from you, but finally there was something that you fought for blindly—the possibility of being alone. When you felt that they were compelling you to be like them, and never get away from their system and their rules, you bit and scratched. The same is true of all your relations with people. When you feel that another personality is impeding the development of your own, you feel an embarrassment which is really the repression of rage.

Of course, there are other reasons arising from this. As long as somewhere in society, in individuals, there are centers of isolation, there is also a possibility of development and change. Fascism is not even an aristocratic form of society in which the people at the top curtain windows in their minds, light within darkness, centers of air and space. They are just the levers which crush the lives below into a solid mass of weight and darkness. I am fighting all the time for the possibility of change. The life I love is now like a warm current in a pond which threatens at any moment to become a solid block of ice.

The Communists say that this is an imperialist war, and, to the usual extent, they are right. But in the old days of about a fortnight ago when they labelled fascism the aggressor, they were still more right. Really it is a war between an imperialism, which is certainly a bad system but which still contains the possibility of change, and an imperialism turned into a kind of madness by Hitler. From an imperialist point of view this war really is unnecessary even to Hitler. He really wants war just as dictators have always wanted some kind of historic climax to their lives.

Well then, if war is madness and Hitler is mad, why reply to madness with madness? Why fight? Why not be a pacifist? The answers are (1) That I am not enough of a mystic to believe that if Hitler won we would not lose the values I care about—the possibility of individual development, artistic creation and social change. (2) That in politics, the possibilities of acting effectively are always limited to certain very definite lines. They are not, as some people imagine, extended to every kind of idealistic and utopian attitude. Given a war, a pacifist is simply a person who has put himself politically out of action, and in so doing is helping the other side. Possibly helping the other side may sometimes further peace, but in this war I don't see how it can. Of course, there is a great deal to be got out of refusing to touch evil, in the way of saving one's own soul and being an example for the future. But actually my personal salvation and getting myself into a morally correct position superior to all my fellow beings do not appeal to me for some reason. If I ran away it would be because I wanted to save my skin or get on with my work, not because I felt that even the world at war was unendurably wicked.

September 5

Oh, but books are crammed with all these arguments. If I started making speeches I would use them, and as I used them I would feel a growing doubt in my own mind about their validity. I would be saying to myself, "Yes, I do, really and truly, believe that, so why is this doubt growing like a fungus in my own mind? Why do I imagine that someone over there in the corner is sniggering? That the man with hair too far back on his temples and wearing a brown tweed jacket knows the answer to everything I am saying? Gradually Conviction is seeping out of the hall like water out of a tank with every word I say."

Doubtless my own contempt for my father's public speeches is what undermines my faith in political arguments. When I start a train of argument it is like the trains on the Berlin Underground which strut confidently above the streets on their raised viaducts, surrounded below by the black tenements which seem to ask whether after all everything is going quite so well as the passengers in the train, flashing through slums, seem to think.

I shall try to recover Germany as it was in 1929-1932, when I lived there for several months of each year. The people I knew there were not like the present rulers of Germany, not like the SS men, not like the army, though I think I understand the army. Germans have a greater capacity, I should say, than any other people for invoking the idea of peace—Ruhe. To us and to the French, peace is a negative state when we are getting on with our business and private lives and are not at war. But to the Germans a state of peace is something positive and breathing and constructive, as opposed to a state of war. The positive idea of peace permeates a great deal of German romantic literature and music. Works like the slow movements of Beethoven's 4th Symphony are hymns to peace. They summon up a vision of a landscape exhaling peace. *Dämmerung* is a peaceful word, and words like "Heim," "Heimat," "Friede," "Ruhe," are loaded with a greater weight of emotion than the corresponding words in other languages. . . .

Perhaps it is that the German landscape is particularly peaceful. I think of the Rhine at evening, the Harz Mountains, the shores of the Alster at Hamburg with the heavy scent of lime blossom on a summer evening.

I have a German relative who is the wife of an U-Boat Commander. They live in Kiel, which has just been bombed. She plays the piano very well. Recently she came to London and she played an early

Beethoven sonata to us at my grandmother's flat. After she had played the slow movement, her face was streaming with tears. "Excuse me," she said, "but the music is so full of peace."

Ten years after the war, Germany was full of peace, it dripped with peace, we swam in peace, no one knew what to do with all the German peace. They built houses with flat roofs, they sunbathed, they walked with linked hands under the lime trees, they lay together in the woods, they talked about art. Above all, everything was new and everyone was young. They liked the English very much and they were sorry about the war. They talked about the terrible time they had had during the inflation.

This was in Hamburg. I used to bathe, and I went to parties of young people. I had never enjoyed parties before and never have since, but these were like living in the atmosphere of a Blue Period Picasso. Everyone was beautiful, and gentle, everyone was poor, no one was smart. On summer evenings they danced in the half-light, and when they were tired of dancing they lay down in the forest, on the beach, on matresses, on the bare floor. They laughed a great deal, smiling with their innocent eyes and showing well-shaped teeth. Sometimes they let one down—sometimes the poorer ones stole, for example—but there was no Sin. I am not being ironic. There really was no sin, like there is in this kind of life in England.

Of course, it was all very superficial; it has all been blown away now. I could not dance. I could not speak German. I stood rather outside it. I think of the sad emigrés who were the exquisite confident students of the Weimar Republican days. Perhaps it was all fictitious, but now in letting the mirage fade from the mind, I get very near to it because everything in Germany is inclined to be fictitious. The German tends to think of his life as an operatic cycle emerging from a series of myths. There was the War, then there was the Inflation, then there was the period of Youth and the Weimar Republic, then there was the Crisis, then there was Hitler. Every German can readily explain him- or herself in terms of What We Have Been Through.

Perhaps[5] we should not laugh at this for isn't really a passive attitude towards life a tendency which we see everywhere, and which provides us with the connection between public events and the breakdown of all standards of private morality? Aren't the dumb oxen, heroes and heroines of modern fiction, doing exactly this?

. . . This passive attitude to life, the tendency to consider oneself a product of circumstances and environment gives one the connection between the breakdown of external standards and the private standards of people. A young man fighting in the Spanish War wrote a poem to his lover beginning:

"Heart of the heartless world."

He was either optimistic or very lucky. I know that a truer line would have been:

"Heartless one of the heartless world."

I was twenty in those days, and I was caught up mostly with the idea of Friendship—*Freundschaft*, which was a very important part of the life of the Weimar Republic. This, if it was frank, was also very idealistic. It was not cynical, shamefaced, smart, snobbish, or stodgy, as so often in England. It was more like Walt Whitman's idea of camaraderie. I admit that I do not feel at all easy about this now, but I set it down for what it was. Two friends, young men, faced the world together: they camped, they travelled, they were happy in each other's company. There was usually a certain casualness about these relationships, a frank admiration of beauty. The Germans had a reputation at that time of being homosexual, but I think it would be truer to say that they were bisexual, though there were of course a few of those zealots and martyrs who really hate women, whom one finds everywhere. But what the young, free, handsome German looked for in the world was a reflection of his own qualities in either man or woman. It was part of the myth that he should "travel light" and have no responsibilities. . . .

A life in which people are exercising sexual freedom without, apparently, anyone suffering or paying for it in any way, is very attractive. One wonders how it is done. In this case, I think it was done at the cost of making everything exist on exactly the same level. The new architecture, the Bauhaus,[6] the social equality, the most casual affairs, marriage, an abortion, a party, were all just the same— they were a pack of cards all of equal value, precariously constructed so that when one fell the whole house came down.

I stayed in Hamburg with a young Jew whom I got to dislike far more than, in retrospect, I think he deserved. I disliked him because he had, as I thought, an attitude towards the life around him as though he were at once watching it from outside and in some way living it. He had a dead, expressionless face, and he listened to what everyone said half as if he were criticizing it, half as if he were thinking, "This is life!" Whilst the others were participating in each other's lives, giving and taking, living and enjoying, he in some way remained an outsider, watching and willing to pick up any scraps of generosity or sex that were thrown his way. He was the only one of the people I knew there who was rich, but he was notoriously stingy. The fact that he had a sophisticated, a collector's, attitude towards this life which I was in love with irritated me intensely. Amongst other things, he collected his own feelings and would murmur of his "affair" with so and so or so and so, five years earlier on.

The young Germans took him much less seriously than I did. "You see, he is a Jew. He can't help it," they would laugh. Being partly Jewish myself, I didn't feel quite easy about this. I told them my mother was of Jewish extraction. They laughed again and said politely, "Oh no, it isn't possible, we don't believe you!" But I had never noticed a Jew being so consciously a Jew as E.

Actually, I think they knew far less about E. than, [after] a few weeks, I did. They regarded Jews as outsiders, without knowing very much about them. But they made the Jews conscious of the fact that they were Jews.

Again and again I had experience of the German ignorance of Jews. Later, when Christopher and I were staying in Insel Ruegen, and when the Nazis were doing exercises every evening in the woods and the "movement" had become a serious menace, I got to know one or two of these young men. They were not gay, irresponsible, intelligent, like the Hamburg set. They were heavy, stupid, but friendly and well-meaning. They seemed perfectly content to lounge round all day sunbathing, listening to the band, going to the dance hall in the evening and having their girls in the pine trees afterward among the hungry mosquitoes. But actually their fun lacked lightness. For instance, when they sunbathed they would build little forts for themselves on the beach, set up a flagpost, hoist a Nazi flag on it and gaze up in reverence. Whilst they were lounging round listening to the music, they seemed always to be waiting for a patriotic air and when one was played they would stand to attention.

I was with two of them on some such occasion as this when I suddenly lost my temper and said, "Ich bin ein Jude!" They laughed incredulously. "You, a Jew? Impossible. Why, you're the perfect Nordic type," said one of them. "You're tall, you have blue eyes, fair hair, Scandinavian features," said the other. "That's why we know and like you." This revelation astonished me. "Then what do you think when you meet a Jew?" I asked. "We want to kill and destroy the pest," they said. "We want to crush him and knock him down." "Then knock me down!" I said. "Here I am. I am a Jew. Please knock me down." They looked at me, dazed by the deceptiveness of this wolf in Nordic clothing. I felt quite sorry for them. Then I got angry. "I don't believe you have any idea what a Jew looks like," I said. "You imagine a monster, when really you have to deal with a human being. I don't believe you know what you are talking about, and your heads are stuffed with stupid hatreds and lies." Probably I didn't know enough German to say all that, but I worked myself up into a great rage and rushed home to laugh with Christopher about it.

On another occasion someone made friends with me in the train specifically because I was of the Nordic type and, indeed, now I know exactly the kind of warm response that a Nordic appearance arouses in some Germans. How can one understand the tremendous interest in appearance of a military race? A uniform face, in a uniform physique, dressed in a uniform, and marching. In a way the Hamburg set who wanted girls to be like boys and everyone to have a lovely face on a perfect body had their craving for uniformity too.

Certainly 1929 was the beginning of the slump and the end of the efflorescence of the Weimar Republic.

September 6th

I want to go on about Germany, about my landlord's Berlin, about Curtius,[7] but I feel too tired, I can't go on. The first thing about any war is that everyone is tired; countries at war are countries of tiredness—fatigue becomes a spiritual experience. Fatigue becomes an illumination. Fetters of habit . . . fall away, and one enters into a more easy relationship with one's fellow beings, an exhausted state of being oneself. The wrong words that come into one's mind and that rigid discipline of wakefulness would reject, are suddenly the right ones. Everything flows freely and nervously; one does not even respect the heavy weight on one's eyes because one seems so much light. . . .

I am humiliated by the need of loving. A few days ago, I dreamt that I had a fight with [Marston]. He looked [anxious] like he does look, and I threw stones at him. I could not throw the stones hard enough; they were very light pebbles, but all the same they hurt him. Then we both fell over and his head became locked in my arm. I felt—as I have felt before in dreams—that I could hurt him infinitely and with that all desire to hurt became pointless. At the same time his face changed into that of someone very beautiful and I woke up feeling pity and love. I did not know whether I was more humiliated by my need of love or my inability to hate.

I remember again the water, the flowing line of the hills, the rich harvest quality of Germany. Immediately, of course, I suspect it of a certain falsity, a certain coarseness and thickness and monotony of texture; but still it is there, there like Wordsworth's poem about the peasant girl.[8] E. took me all over the place. His relationship with me was a sustained kind of mental seduction. He had a little car, and when he wasn't watching the road his eyes were on me watching the effects of the storks on North German villages, of monkeys masturbating at the Hagenbeck zoo, of the Harz Mountains. "If you like music, we shall have a great deal in common," he said when we first met. And if ever I admitted for one moment that I appreciated anything, his eyes were ready to smile, "Ah, we have a great deal in common."

So we went to the Harz Mountains, stopping on our way at Brunswick where we saw in a very dusty and deserted gallery one of the finest Rembrandts I have ever seen. We visited some people called Harman who had a house in the Harz Mountains. Like everyone else, they had lost their money and all they had was the property itself and, I suppose, the salary of Professor Harman. The whole family, grandfather, son, daughter-in-law, a grandson, two daughters, and a brother and sister who were fellow students of Wolfgang, the son, were there. Like nearly everyone I met in Germany at this time, they were obviously living from hand to mouth. They spent what they had; they laughed and talked a great deal and yet they had an air of having lost everything. Wolfgang had rather pinched, vague features which had a certain pallid, distracted beauty which attracted me very much at the time. He was very much worried about sex, and at night he would walk with a vague expression into the bedroom of Fräulein Bindler, the sister of the student. She received him into bed, but was afraid of having a child. I am sure that everyone knew about this, and in some comforting way thought it was right, or at all events just accepted it. He was also concerned with other problems than sex—philosophy, poetry, art—and walked round the uncared-for garden ernestly discussing Maurois' *Byron*[9] with me.

E. spent the whole afternoon and evening remorselessly asking to be put up for the night. "Oh, but we can share a room quite easily," he said. "In fact," with a quick smile at me, "we should rather *like* to share a room." They seemed to regard him as a joke. "He is a Jew," they evidently thought. "He is an Englishman." And they liked the English. They played a word game in which the clues turned out to be a rather unkind joke on E.'s name. But they laughed.

Several years later, after Hitler's rise to power, Wolfgang came to visit me in London. Earnest and pale as ever, he had a mission: he wanted to convert me to Nazism. "Of course, there are things I do not like about them," he said. "I do not agree with their views on literature and art. I do not sympathize with the persecution of the Jews. I do not accept their explanation of the Reichstag fire. But all the same they have a faith." Here his fists clenched and his eyes burned with a rather questioning mystery. "They have restored to us our belief in Germany and in life. Some of them are idealists. There is a great deal of socialism in their Germany." I raged as I had done before. I said, "If I were a German, as I well might be, I would now be either in a concentration camp or else deprived of any means of earning my living. You can't expect me to be fair. I don't care about your reasons." . . .

This was an unnecessary piece of self-righteousness on my part, because I heard later that he became disillusioned about the Nazis and was one of those unhappy, pained, gentle creatures who represent the heart of another Germany, and do not understand what is happening to them. I have touched a deeper chord than I knew here, for have I not met two or three of them? Don't I know very well the peculiar whiteness and stillness of their eyes which seem to have been drained of pigment? These poor ghosts are really beautiful in a sexless way, because, if one is a young man of another era, naturally one cannot expect to be virile. How closely I press now upon a secret! Why am I always attracted by these desolate spirits? There was one whom I met on the Hook of Holland boat once, shortly before Hitler's rise to power. He was the son of a general, and now that at least four names crowd onto me, I remember that they are all aristocrats and often close to the higher ranks of the army. I cannot remember the names exactly. Oh yes, this boy was called Horst. He had a round face with very well-formed features, delicate lips, light blue eyes, and brown hair of an almost feathery lightness. He was very quiet and polite, and he had some small, out-of-the-way interest—playing the flute or making musical instruments or something. There's really nothing much more to it than that. He had a scholarship at Oxford and I used to call on him there; we went for walks and I introduced him to Isaiah Berlin. But he never in the least became part of the life at Oxford. He was always just as gentle, just as isolated, and gradually one saw beyond the varnish of his interest in the musical instrument—or whatever—to a distress and restlessness of spirit that never ceased. Berlin saw him several times and then confessed to me that the sustained gentle sense of his unhappiness was too much: he no longer cared for him.

Another such was surely Jowo von Molke, who wandered about Europe looking at pictures. They all had some mild objective interest which obviously was not their life, but which covered their refusal ever to speak about Germany. Perhaps, like Wolfgang, when the Nazis first came to power they flamed with momentary hope which soon disappeared as they reverted to their former hobby. . . .

But the most remarkable case was the young aristocrat I met in Isaiah Berlin's room only a few months ago. He was a Prussian and his name was Jobst. He had the fine looks of all those well-bred Germans, though in his case something seemed to have gone wrong. There was the blonde hair, the blue eyes, the well-defined bones and strong jaw, and yet in spite of its fine structure his face seemed to have collapsed. Perhaps his mouth when in repose was almost too rich and well-formed, and when he moved it seemed to become distorted, and the lips to disappear altogether. He was tall and strongly built, but his movements were so nervous and the veins of his hands stood out so much and were yet so fine, that he had the appearance of being pulled the whole time by hundreds of strands of fine cord. We talked about music, for which he had an immense passion. I remember that we discussed love in music for some reason. I forget what composer he thought best expressed love, but I know it was not Beethoven. Perhaps it was Monteverdi in "Ardo." But the idea of Germany hung over us because he was going back there the next morning. His mother who was travelling with him was waiting somewhere a few doors away.

We stayed up till three o'clock, Isaiah and Jobst talking without stopping. I got very sleepy, so sleepy that I lay down on the sofa and attempted to doze from time to time. But the spirits of Horst, of Adam von Trott, of Wolfgang Harman, of Jowo von Molke were pacing the room and would not let me rest. He did not really attempt to apologize as he said, "Excuse me for keeping you up, but we shall never meet again." "Oh nonsense," said Isaiah. "No, no. It is not nonsense. We shall never meet again. I know it. This is my last day of peace." He did not say anything about Germany. He only said, "It is very sad I leave Oxford. I shall never see anything of this again." Then he started once more on to music, illustrating his conversation by singing and conducting with his hands.

Next morning, he turned up again before breakfast. "I have not slept," he said. "I went to bed at three, lay down for three hours, and got up at six." "Why did you get up at six?" I asked. "Because it is my last morning, and I shall never see all this again." He held out his long, expressive, nervous right hand. Other people called, but even when Jobst was silent, it was really impossible to escape from his drama. He did not rest. When he stopped pacing round the room, he knelt down with those speaking hands of his touching the carpet. The worst of it was that he was not an actor. He was by nature a quiet, scholarly person with a rich inner drama. Seeing him out was as unexpected and shocking as, say, seeing one's father cry.

September 8th

When I consider it, the trouble with all the nice people I knew in Germany is that they were tired or weak. The young people in Hamburg were tired, the young Nationalist aristocrats were weak. How are the people of good will today to avoid weakness and fatigue?

September 9th

Yesterday morning while I was waiting for a bus, some soldiers passed down the road singing "It's a long long way to Tipperary." An unshaved and very ragged old tramp wearing the ribbons of several medals so loosely attached to his coat that they were almost falling off, said to me, "They're singing now, but they won't be singing when they come back. Hearing 'em sing reminds me of when I went to fight in the trenches. We went out singing, but we didn't sing for long."

In the afternoon I got a taxi to Waterloo before going into the country. We were stopped near Southampton Row by five Frenchmen carrying a flag and singing the "Marseillaise." The taximan said to me, "They won't be doing that for long."

Hugh Gibb told me that during an air raid warning he went into a shelter in Hyde Park. After a quarter of an hour he was bored, came up and walked to the Round Pound. An elderly woman came tripping over the grass, singing. "Do you know why I'm singing?" she asked. "I'm singing because I'm happy." She threw some crumbs to some sparrows and said, "Come on, my treasures. The animals don't care about air raids. They're not afraid of being killed in ten minutes. Yet do you know what animal has to pay to exist?" "No," said Hugh. "A dog," she said. "A dog has to pay ten shillings a year to exist. Yet those miserable creatures huddled underground a few yards from here won't even provide the dogs, who pay 10/- a year for a license to exist, with gas masks. Come on my treasures," she said, feeding the sparrows and went off singing.

Peter Watson traveled from Paris to Calais two days ago in a troop train. The compartment was crowded with soldiers. They sat all the way in absolute silence, no one saying a word.

There is very little cheering this war. There is no talk of victory. It is a war simply to avoid defeat, and to end the suspense of the last few years with war always hanging over us. The most hopeful thing is this complete lack of desire for a resounding triumph. Get rid of Hitler and then let the Germans do what they like is what people seem to think.

September 10th

"The best lack all conviction, while the worst are full of passionate intensity."[10] W. B. Yeats, who wrote these lines, himself became a Fascist sympathizer. He was prepared to accept the worst; he wanted strength at any price.

Why were the gentle and kind people I knew in Germany tired or weak?

The tiredness of our generation consists of exploring unimportant and superficial aspects of the idea of freedom. Freedom, the young people in Hamburg said, is sexual freedom primarily, then freedom to enjoy yourself, to "wander," not to make money, not to have the responsibilities of a family or the duties of a citizen, generally. Freedom is one long holiday. They were tired. What they wanted, in fact, was a holiday.

After 1929, it became obvious that the world of these people was threatened.

New styles of architecture, a change of heart. The architecture was mostly swimming baths built with money raised from American loans. The change of heart, sunbathing and sexual freedom, was almost as uneconomical an investment as the new architecture. That's to say, although it produced a charming little shoot, it didn't really take root in the very strong and barren soil of the post-war years.

I feel uneasy about discussing these things in a Left Book Club manner, suddenly identifying myself with the Workers in order to sneer at the people whom I meet for coffee, and dismissing my own past as though I have renounced it finally. The fact is that my own sex and life is very unsatisfactory. I have just had a first-class failure in my personal life, and I am so full of regret and bitterness that I dream of nothing else.

However, important as these things are, the first sign of the German tiredness is to treat them as though nothing else was more important. My friends in Hamburg behaved as though nothing mattered in life except sex and personal relationships, and at the same time they kept these problems in a state of perpetual, unsolved, pleasurable suspense.

But if a human relationship becomes more important than anything else in two people's lives, it simply means that there is a lack of trust between these two human beings. A relationship is not a way of entering into a kind of dual subjectivity, a redoubled and reciprocal egotism; it is an alliance of two people who form an united front to deal with the problems of the objective world. The problem of married people is not to become absorbed in each other, but how not to become absorbed in each other; how, in a word, to trust one another in order to enter into a strong and satisfactory relationship with the outside world.

A great cause of weakness with people today is putting less important things before those that are more important—for example, personal relations before work and an objective philosophy of life, sex before love. People who put personal relations before their tasks in society become parasites on each other, form mutual admiration societies, agree to do nothing that will give one a social advantage over the other, and prevent each other from doing so. People who put sex before love perpetually flee from one marital relationship to another because, for them, sex has become a thing in itself dissociated from personal relationships. They have an image in their mind of 100% sexual satisfaction, and when they are in love they are continually asking themselves, "Am I satisfied?"; they are continually tormented by the thought that perhaps they are not. For them love, at first an opportunity, soon becomes a trap, preventing them from enjoying the possibly greater delights that they might get elsewhere.

Satisfactory personal relationships exist when the people who enjoy them have a satisfactory relation with society. They exist within society; they are not a conspiracy against society. In the same way, satisfactory sex exists within love and it can be attained through love, which means patience and loyalty and understanding.

Another cause of weakness is not to admit, but to pursue our failures blindly. There is such a thing as real failure in personal relationships and in sex. How easily, then, that which symbolizes failure, the poor substitute improvised for love, becomes the most important thing in life! How people build it up and call the scars of failure their dazzling successes! Masturbation, homosexuality, following people in the streets, breaking up relationships because one has failed in one's own, all these compensatory activities form a circle of Hell in which people can never rest from proving that their failures are the same as love. Yet the lives of countless men and women show that the great compensation lies in [recognizing] failures as failures, and substitutes as substitutes, making the most of the rest of one's life. In fact, the great artists and figures in literature have almost without exception been failures in life. By this I mean that their relations with their fellow beings were really and truly at some point unsatisfactory, that most of them were fully conscious of this, and that their honesty in admitting a defect restored to their lives a sense of scale which hopelessly neurotic people lack. Baudelaire' relationship with a negress, the breakdown of Gauguin's marriage which led him to the South Seas, Van Gogh's failures in love, Rilke's wanderings and sense of unfulfilment, to mention only a few examples which immediately come to mind, were all real failures in life, and to the "man of genius" the failure to be a complete man must always be a humiliation. The compensations of genius are so dazzling that it is difficult for outsiders to realize that Beethoven and Balzac suffered when they yet had the tremendous privilege of being Beethoven and Balzac. They suffered as men; they rejoiced as creators.

The creative artist realizes that art is not a complete life, otherwise he would really be self-sufficient; he would be cut off from the world and there would be happy, unreal artists creating a truly pure art. Some people, who are not artists, or who are bad artists, think that art is like this, a world completely cut off from the world, where esthetic experience is everything. These are the virtuosi of art and of appreciation, spirits which have flowed completely into an esthetic medium, without the friction of living their lives.

Of all the arts, music provides the most self-complete alternative world removed from the real world. Painting is the most objective of the arts because visual imagery always has a direct reference to seen objects. In order to get away from the sane, broad day, painters have deliberately to paint their visual experiences remembered from sleep—nightmares. But music is not a dream that imitates our sleep; it is a world of its own, full of abstract aural patterns which are not related to the noises we hear in every day life. At the same time it creates a world of tremendous emotional conviction. The absolute ideas which have such a wavering meaning in words and which it puzzles us to attach to human behavior have their fixed places in music. Schiller's *Ode to Liberty* is a work which conveys little more to us today than a sense of enthusiasm for ideas which meant a great deal to Schiller but which the time between him and us has cast a doubt, if not a slur, on. But in the music of the last movement of Beethoven's Ninth Symphony these ideas are fixed in a world of their own which one can enter without referring it back to the real world and the disillusion of the past hundred years.

Actually, the value of the music lies in the fact that it does nevertheless refer back to the real world of experience. The triumph of art is not merely a triumph over technical difficulties, but the triumph of resolving the conflicts of life into an eduring form of acceptance and contemplation. To regard these great arts of acceptance—the masterpieces of art—as acts of rejection and escape is simply a way of losing grip; it is letting the engine run without the wheels turning. If one looks at the faces of people at a concert, one can see the difference between those who use music as a form of living and those who use it as a form of dying. The virtuoso of listening is, like the virtuoso of performing, a wonderful child, one who has never grown up but melted himself on the furnace of works of art where he continually flows away. The people who are not just virtuosi have a certain sculptural rigidity—the face of Schnabel or Toscanini—because they are always discovering a unity between the experiences of life and of art.

The young aristocratic sons of German militarists whom I call "weak" were trying, without much conviction, it is true, to use the appreciation of art as a complete way of living, and as an escape from their despair about Germany. But this does not work. You go to the concert and music offers an interior life of sounds inside your head which is as complete as anything you have experienced. You read a play of Shakespeare and you enter into a love and a courage of feeling completer because more explicit and final than anything your own life may provide. "This is real for me; everything else can be put aside and forgotten." But it can't. The felt life in the work of art is only intense, and often painful, because it actually touches the life of deep and terrible experience. Without this experience art would simply express a tendency towards perfection. But in works of art there is a real conflict of life, a real breaking up and melting down of intractable material, feelings and sensations which seem expressionless lumps of experience until they have been transformed into art. A work of art doesn't say, "I am life. I offer you the opportunity of becoming me." On the contrary, it says, "This is what life is like. It is even realer—less to be evaded—than you thought. But I offer you an example of acceptance and understanding. Now, go back and live!"

September 12th

Today I applied for a job as a translator in the War Office. Yesterday I had a printed slip from the Ministry of Information saying that my name was on a list of writers who may be used later. But I don't think I have a chance as I am told that that Ministry is very overcrowded with applicants. Nor do I think the War Office will want me, as there must be many translators far better qualified. I feel that perhaps I ought to be doing stretcher work or filling sandbags or something and perhaps later I shall volunteer for one of these. But as long as I can write and read a good deal each day, I am not really bothering. What I would like most is to complete three books: this journal, a novel, and a book of poems before I am called up.

Lunched with Joe Ackerley who was depressed, having dined the evening before with someone high up in the Ministry of Information. He said that our achievement so far in the war was to have bombed a Danish village, shot down two Belgian planes, shot down one British plane during the last air-raid alarm, and lost five other planes which simply dived into the sea during the raid on the Canal.

I want to remember all I can about Ernst Robert Curtius.

Of course, E. in Hamburg was exactly what I mean by a passively watching and listening virtuoso in his attitude to the life around him. He lived his life through other people, forming a kind of legend out of their lives in which he could forget his own disappointments. He collected people in a dead way, much as some people collect furniture or works of art to which they can pay a respect which they feel they do not owe to themselves. One of his chief pleasures was in introducing interesting people to each other in order that he might enjoy their reactions and also have the pleasure of giving to one friend another friend; in his wretched humility he felt that he had so little to give of himself. Not possessing himself, he possessed and gave away his friends.

For some reason, he became very excited at the idea of Ernst Robert and me meeting. He therefore arranged that I should go specially to Baden Baden in order to meet Ernst Robert. What I find difficult to explain is my own willingness to fall in with this proposal. . . .

This thought did not trouble me. I simply got out of the train, booked a room in a hotel and, as soon as I had washed, walked straight to the house where Curtius was staying. I do not remember the details; I only remember the feeling of that first meeting. As far as I can recall, the house was outside the town and I had to walk some way along a road past various hotels, and then along a path through the edge of the woods before I came to the house. I think that I was shown into a room on the first floor, and perhaps there was a cool meal with fruit and wine laid on a table with a white cloth spread over it. There were bay windows opening onto a balcony, and a pleasant freshness of the forest at evening filled the room. Everything, I think, gave me an impression of coolness, and for some reason I thought that the host and hostess were ill. The host, whose name I never knew, was dressed in a white suit, and both he and his wife seemed pale.

I did not stay long enough to get to know them for Curtius immediately stepped forward, grasped my hand firmly and told his friends that he would go to a Bierhalle in Baden with me.

Railway journeys have a discomforting effect on me. They stimulate me so much that all my usual impressions seem to flow much faster, with the train, like a film that is shown very quickly. I cannot check this. In spite of myself, every sort of sensation pours through my brain during a train journey, and when I was younger and playing at "thinking books," a project for some unwritten novel or play would force all its images onto me during a journey. This excess of stimulation leaves me afterwards in a state of drugged tiredness in which I appear stupid to myself and either am able to talk very revealingly, or else get muddled in everything I say. I was in this mood that first evening and I talked very freely and indiscreetly to Ernst Robert about my life in Hamburg.

He listened to me with an amusement which slightly, yet affectionately, was laughing at me as well as with me. In my deepest friendships—with Auden, with Christopher Isherwood, and with Curtius—I have been conscious of being thus taken "with a pinch of salt." . . . Sometimes it is disconcerting to be laughed at when one is serious, but as long as it is done affectionately one is grateful to people who enable one to see oneself a little from the outside. From the first, Ernst Robert's attitude to me was one of gentle raillery, and I think that because he saw so far beyond me and at the same time loved me, I owe more to him than to any other older person.

Being anxious to impress him, I talked about literature, and especially about Dostoievsky, whom I was reading. I was very interested in madness, partly because at school and Oxford I had been taught to regard myself as mad, and because Auden who, when he was an undergraduate was anxious to maintain a certain superiority over his contemporaries, always treated me as a lunatic. Experiences like my cerebral excitement on train journeys, my excessive credulity, my lack of a complete understanding with even my best friends so that I always felt they stood to some extent outside me, bore out my theory of my own madness. Above all, I was, like everyone, in search of that ecstasy which is so lacking in our civilization that even war and violence are to some people a secret consolation in a world of dull routine governed by material values—that ecstasy which is the justification of every kind of adventure and unscrupulousness in private lives. In Hamburg E., with his collector's zeal, had discovered a mad expressionist artist, a woman with a real talent for drawing, recently released from a lunatic asylum where she had done some really terrifying portraits of the lunatics. She had done a portrait of me, making me look wild and mad. I was very proud of this and took Ernst Robert back to my room to see it. But so far from being impressed or interested, he would scarcely look at it. He said that it was mad and that I did not need to be mad.

During the next few days, I walked with him in the Black Forest. We went swimming together. We drank beer every evening. He criticized Dostoievsky; he told me to read other things than the Russians, particularly the French. I showed him poems I had written and, to my surprise, instead of reading them with the patronizing superiority of one immersed in the greater literature of the world, he read them with evident delight, and made some translations of them which were [later] published in the *Neue Schweizer Rundschau*. He listened to my accounts of my life in Hamburg, and scandalized me by treating this life which I thought so highly of simply as pornography in which he was unashamedly interested. But to him it was pornography; it was not, as it seemed to me . . . ecstasy.

September 15th

I spent most of yesterday and the day before typing this journal out and writing a review of Dylan Thomas's *Map of Love*. [11] I shall try to work this journal into a book with several levels of time, present and past, which I am able to move in as I choose. During these first days of the war, and first days of the breaking up of my marriage, I tend to live in the past, partly because the present is so painful, partly because it is so fragmentary and undecided. We live in a kind of vacuum at present in which the events on which we are waiting have not yet caught up on us, though our hour is very near. We have seen this whirlwind in China, in Central Europe, in Spain, in Poland, and now we are next on the list. If I let my mind drift on the present, I have terrible day dreams. Last night, walking the streets in the blackout, I had one of an aggressive alliance between Germany and Russia, which would not only destroy the whole of the rest of Europe, but divide it utterly on questions of principle. Another of my unpleasant day dreams is a growing fear that this is only the first of a series of wars. This fear springs from the following reflections. Supposing the Allies win the war, what kind of peace will they make? The answer is that they must either repeat the mistakes of the Treaty of Versailles, or else they must establish Germany as a strong power under military dictatorship.

I think that this time they will probably plump for the military dictatorship. What they hope for, I am sure, is a military coup in Germany, whereby the generals will get rid of Hitler and sue for peace. A smashing victory for the Allies would mean a complete internal collapse in Germany, followed by a communist revolution backed by Russia, and probably a war of reactionary intervention which would be boycotted by the workers here and in France. I am sure they do not want that. They are hoping that the military caste in Germany will be pacifist and reactionary. But I fear that they are wrong. Hitler has really transformed and stupefied Germany into a military camp, and we must choose between a socialist Germany and a more or less permanent state of war. The factor of modern armament is in favor of a permanent state of war between great countries who will completely swallow up the small countries. The little states will disappear, and the great states will remain invulnerable behind their Maginot and Siegfried Lines and their balloon barrages until there is a complete collapse and they destroy each other.

Imperialist wars used to have objectives which could be attained without one country completely ruining the other. Colonies were grabbed, indemnities paid, territories curtailed, and the great powers went on living side by side. But now there is really no objective except the complete destruction of one power by another. Every return to some status quo, say 1914, or 1918, or 1933, or 1937, is simply a way of putting the clock back so that the struggle may start again to the advantage of whatever country was best off at the time.

Therefore, no one who is fighting for a realignment of the forces of national power is fighting for a just order. All we are fighting for is self-preservation, when less and less becomes worth preserving, in a life-or-death struggle between Empires which are bent on destroying each other.

Supposing there was an affirmative alliance between Stalin and Hitler on the understanding that Germany was socialized. You would then get a revolution dictated to the rest of Europe by the combined fleets of Russia and Germany, and the most rigid tyranny and suppression of all personal opinion. In the long run, it might be a good thing because at any rate it would mean the breakdown of this tragic cycle of rival nationalisms. But it would mean the surrender of everything we call freedom in our lifetime. If such a combination occurred, I think I would become a pacifist, because nothing would then seem to me worth fighting for.

I do not think these speculations are of much value; it's better to get back to the little world I have some concrete understanding of, and the only point in giving rein to the nightmare is to preserve a sense of proportion. To show I am aware of the fact that the life of myself and mine is like Lear's hut on the moor in the thunderstorm, and filled with madness from within and outside. . . .

[I know at least] a dozen people [who are] worse off than I; so I should not complain. There is Fini whose brother is fighting on the other side. There is John [Lehmann] whose friend Toni is in an Austrian division. There are one or two Germans I know who have been interned. The whole of Europe is filled with people who are violently separated from those they love, whose homes and children are torn from them, who search for their possessions in a heap of ashes. Compared with these brutal realities, my luxury marriage and luxury separation seem an extravagant game of people who are millionaires in the way they spend their feelings. I ought to be glad to be alone and away from this nonsense. Perhaps in the next few years it is only people who are alone who will be able to try to put their minds in order and realize what is going on round them. . . .

September 18th

Spent the weekend at Rogate in Sussex. Marvellous weather, very hot indeed. On Sunday heard the news of Russia coming into the war. Although I expected this, it is so contrary to my hopes that it came as a great shock. It makes nonsense of the Russian policy of opposing aggressors, which they have upheld during the past ten years. The Communists here describe it as a great blow against Germany. But when the Non-Aggression Pact between Germany and Russia was signed, they said there would be an escape clause excluding aggression. When there was no such clause, they then said that it was at any rate a tremendous blow to the Axis, particularly Japan. Since then Japan has concluded an alliance with Russia. Two days ago the leadership of the American C.P. was reported in the press by saying that this was an imperialist war, and it was necessary to remain isolated and neutral. However, this is not the policy of the English Communists who are all for helping Poland.

One can easily imagine the British Government becoming almost as Fascist as its opponents as a result of this war. In that case, everything we are fighting for and against is reduced to nonsense, as are also the divisions between Communist and Fascist in each country. Democracy, Communism, and Fascism are simply names for three brands of Imperialism. I do not say that this has happened or even will happen. All I mean is that if one attempts to attach oneself to any political party or any warring interest, one may have the ground cut away from one's feet completely. Therefore, whilst I certainly remain as opposed to Fascism as ever I was, I think it is necessary to practice a certain detachment; that is, to work out a system of values for oneself which one can fall back on if civilization becomes completely chaotic.

Today I met Pears in the street. We discussed the Russian coup, and he said that the whole situation made him wish to have to go, in order that he might then be able to examine all the relevant documents and discover what has really happened between Hitler and Stalin. He is right. When our lives are threatened, the most sensible thing is to start living as though one could see beyond the darkness of the tunnel into the light outside. However much one becomes involved in the struggle from day to day, one must have a long term view of the final issues for civilization, and also for reconstructing people's personal lives. Politics alter from day to day, and therefore lack continuity; for this reason private life and personal standards become very important because they have a continuity which one mustn't allow to be broken up by outside events.

The Communists argue that by making a pact with Germany, the Russians have broken the Axis and robbed Germany of her Allies. If one applies the same argument to Russian intervention in Spain, one could say that by supporting the Republic the Russians provided a triumph for Franco by splitting up the supporters of the Republic in capitalist democracies. [But at the time] this was not the reason anyone offered for Russian intervention.

September 19th

With Curtius I was in contact with the Germany of Goethe, Hölderlin, and Schiller. That is an Apollonian Germany, a Germany of the sun, not the Dionysian Germany of Hitler who rouses himself from a torpid dullness into a wild frenzy of words and actions. After the war and the blockage, perhaps even the Germans who lay with no clothes on, crucified by the sun, expressed the need for a Germany of "Light—more Light."

It was not the madness of Hölderlin that Curtius liked, but the peaceful development of a poem such as "Brot und Wein," in which the sun-steeped and vine-bearing German landscape is lifted at the end of the poem into a unity with the German conception of Greece. We read Hölderlin together and later on the poems of the Greek Anthology, particularly the erotic ones. . . .

Curtius was an egotist of the liberal, Goethe tradition. His life was organized with an enlightened selfishness; he did not take more than he could take, nor give more than he could give. He would not put himself out, even for his best friends, if he thought that his own resilience was going to be depressed by their needs. One could say, perhaps, that he was a fair weather friend. Once when I was hard up, I wrote asking him if he could introduce me to people in Berlin to whom I could teach English. He wrote back about other things, ending his letter with the curt, "leider kann ich keine Verbindungen für Ihnen im Berlin schaffen."[12] I asked a friend of his, Dr. Moering, about this, and he told me how at a period of crisis and confusion in his life, Ernst Robert had cut himself off from him. I myself have a tendency in my relationships with people never to refuse anything and often to undertake far more than I can undertake. I know how this leads to a feeling of resentment which affects one's relationships with [them], and to a fear of making new acquaintances, who may plunge one into new commitments. He remained happy and light and broad and objective. He would lose this by identifying himself with others in their predicaments.

I do not mean that he was unsympathetic, but that he was unselfsacrificing because what he had was of too great an objective value to himself and to others to sacrifice. He did not enter into their lives because his generosity lay in the freedom with which they could enter into his.

If one accepted this, he gave a great deal.

Once when I was staying at Bonn, I went into Cologne for a night and got into an extremely unpleasant scrape. I liked going to very squalid places, and I went to a hotel near the railway station in the lowest part of town. When I got into bed, I didn't notice that the lock of the door was on the outside instead of the inside, so that the guests in this hotel were like prisoners locked into their rooms instead of guests who could lock out intruders. In the middle of the night, the door was flung open and a man came into the room who put his hands to my throat and threatened to throttle me unless I gave him my money. He was much stronger than I was, and I was undressed, so I asked him to pass me my clothes. He did this, and I gave him my money. It amounted to about 60 or 70 marks, which he did not seem to think enough, so he said he would take my coat as well. I protested about this, but it did not seem much use, so I asked him to leave me a mark at least to pay my fare back to Bonn. He flung a mark down on the marble-topped table beside my bed, and ran out of the room. I lay in bed staring into the darkness and listening to the noises from outside of whores talking and screaming, and a continuous sound like water running away in the darkness. I felt as though I had reached the goal of something horrible and mysterious in my life, as though it were unfolded from my own flesh and was a part of me. I did not resent the theft because I thought of it as something I had let myself in for. I did not blame the thief at all, for what had happened seemed an automatic consequence of my choosing this kind of life and, in short, I felt completely passive, as though a whole process which I had called into being by my own actions were now happening to me, and I knew that I would never escape from it. Because I knew this, it was very difficult for me to resist, but at last I realized that I must do something; so I sat up in bed and shouted for the landlord. A few minutes later, he and two or three other men came into the room, switching on the light, and standing round my bed as though I were an invalid, seriously ill, and they were four specialists whom I had summoned. "Why are you making such a noise in my hotel?" asked the landlord. "I shall call the police." "For heaven's sake, do call the police," I answered, feeling that I was now prepared for any kind of disgrace. "I would like to speak to them very much." This seemed to make him hesitate, and he said quite kindly, "Why, what do you want then?" "Someone in your hotel has just stolen all my money," I said. "This is a disgrace," said the landlord, "I won't have things like this going on in my hotel. Why should you come here and bring this disgrace on me?" "It isn't my fault," I answered. "I am very sorry. I don't mind my money being stolen, but I must have my coat and an assurance that all my clothes won't be stolen, else I won't be able to get home." "Nothing else will be stolen," said the landlord honorably, "I can assure you of that." "Well, might I at least have my coat back?" I asked. He nodded to one of the other men who left the room and returned a few seconds later with my coat. Then he said, "Good night," reassuringly, and they left the room.

I felt that nothing else was likely to happen, but I could not sleep and continued to lie with my eyes open in my waking nightmare. At last it was dawn. Then for the first time it occurred to me that when I arrived the previous night I had been made to pay my bill before taking my room. Therefore, there was not the slightest reason why I should stay any longer. It surprised me to realize that I was free and that nothing final had happened. I quickly put on my clothes and ran downstairs and out of the hotel, without anyone stopping me. I ran until I came to the river. Outside it was cold and raw. In the gray light the cathedral and the bridges and the modern exhibition building had a photographic quality. Suddenly I started laughing. I had a gay sensation of release, and from hating and feeling ashamed I was suddenly dear to myself.

After an hour or so of waiting, I went back to Bonn. When I had rested and changed, I called on Ernst Robert, partly to borrow some money from him. When he saw that I was disturbed, he took me for a walk by the Rhine. Full of shame again, I told him my story. But to my surprise, instead of being shocked, disappointed or upset, he started laughing; putting his arm round me, he patted my shoulder. . . .

While I have been writing this last page and a half, I have had the wireless on, playing Hitler's latest speech. His voice varies from a cavernous rumbling to the peaks of an exalted hysteria from which he shrieks like a raucous beast of prey, until the whole chorus of his followers break into a strong night's thunder of triumphant hatred. Undoubtedly there is something disintegrating about that voice, that applause, and everything they stand for. The cities of one's mind seem to be bombarded, as though a threat could make them fall to pieces. He speaks of a new, terrible secret weapon which, if the English oppose him, he will use. When he does this, I feel as though the world could be destroyed by pressing a button, and he were a madman who had access to this button and was about to press it.

I go to the gramophone and play "Agnus Dei" and "Et in Spiritum" from Bach's Mass in B Minor. During the weekend in Sussex, I played Glück's Orpheus. Reality and exaltation lie in these transparent harmonies, not in the violence and high shrieks of hysteria. One need not ever be afraid that destruction is the real world. Destruction is the real world broken. It is quite possible that I shall be broken and unable to understand Glück's wonderfully formative and coherent music any longer. The part of my mind that composes itself . . . when I hear this music will be a cathedral that has been bombed. But that is no tragedy; it is only an accident. It would only be a tragedy if the destructive form of a life and a civilization which has met with decay were the final and complte goal of man, instead of the broken fragments of an experiment which has been discarded.

September 26
During the fast few days until the weekend, I have been writing my novel. [13]

Today and yesterday, I have had very bad colitis, which makes me unwilling to work. I haven't had it so badly since I was in Greece. On Saturday night I was wakened repeatedly by it, and when I did sleep I had very bad dreams. Inflammation of the intestines makes one have the most oppressive nightmares.

I have not heard from Inez since I saw her, nor have I written to her; I thought I would let her be the first to write this time. Although it is

desolating not to hear, I think it is better than crushing myself by
writing about three letters which would have the effect of bringing
me from her. I had better realize the full extent of her indifference, or I
will live in a condition of illusion in which I really feel insecure. If she
wants me for any reason, I shall doubtless hear from her, but the fact
that I want to hear won't ever bring any kind of response. The sooner I
realize that, the better. One is isolated if the response one does get
from a lover is only a reflex action from one's own love that one
invests in her. I mean one letter for three written to her; still I would
like to forge this complaint in one of those kisses which again seal up
one's security.

Last week I bought a printing press for £5, which was being sold
second hand at a bookshop near here. I have taken it to Bobby Buhler's
flat, and we hope to print small books of poems, stories, etc. by
unknown poets with it. . . .

On Thursday I lunched with Tom Eliot. Friday George Barker[14]
dined here. On Saturday lunched with Peter and the Buhlers at the
Café Royal. Spent the weekend with Leonard and Virginia Woolf.
Also lunched Friday with Goldschmidt.

All these people whom I met last week were concerned with the
work they are going to do during the war, and their attitude to it.

September 29th
. . . In the afternoon I went to Bobby Buhler's and set up type of
one of Bernard's poems. A painter called. Basil Johnson was there.
He is the first person I have met who is very warlike, though he was
only funny about it. He said he disliked all this; we love the
Germans and we only hate Hitler propaganda. He is quite prepared,
he said, to hate the Germans, though until now he has never
thought about them, etc., etc. He wants to join up, and is very sick
of having nothing to do. He was sacked from A.R.P. work, because
when a Duchess came round to inspect their unit, she stopped at
him and said, "What do you do all day, my man?" He answered,
"Play cards."

Dined with Jack Barker, Buhlers, Rodney Philips, and one or two
other people I didn't know. I sabotaged a plan to go to Limehouse. Met
Cyril and spent much of the evening discussing his project for a

magazine.[15] He seemed rather vague about what it would cost—I think it may be more than he imagines. We spent a long time thinking of names, all signs of the zodiac being discussed. The most favoured names were Sirius, Scorpio, Equinox, Centaur, though we really aren't satisfied with any of these. I said I would give him any amount of help but did not want my name used as it has been used too much in this sort of way.

Later in the evening, I went to a party at Rodney's. I talked a lot to Judy Gooseus, who is a marvellously beautiful and intelligent girl who has the sparkling eyes and smiling lips of a girl in a Russian novel. She enters the life of everyone she meets with the untouched enthusiasm and straining excitement of a fish entering fresh waters.

. . . This morning the news about the Russo-German mutual assistance Pact came over the wireless.[16] Although I expected this, I felt shattered when I actually heard it. We are living at a time when we see the forces behind events, and the direction which may take years to be revealed, with a blinding clarity. The question does arise: What are we fighting for? Though this is not quite in the form the Germans put it to us, as in any case we aren't fighting for Poland.

September 30th

The *Times* this morning answers my question by saying that we are fighting for the independence of a new Polish State with an entrance to the sea, and, I suppose, the loss of the bits of Poland which have already gone to Russia.

Yet, if the whole of Eastern Europe is held between the nutcrackers of Russia and Germany, it becomes absurd to talk about fighting for the sovereignty of all these little reactionary states which, anyhow, have been the cause of so many wars. There may be no military alliance between Germany and Russia; they may even hate each other. But whether they love or hate each other, they are now clinched, and no amount of wishful thinking can pretend that they won't destroy any [country] between them that comes in their way.

The probability is that Germany will come more and more under Russian influence as her militarized state and economy becomes more and more socialized. This process would probably absorb all the near-Eastern countries. Then our war would develop into a war of intervention against a revolutionary situation in Central Europe. At the same time, the war in its present early stages will provide the impetus for such a revolution.

The English Communists have now twisted again and say we should make peace and accept what they call "the Russian Terms." I think that they are probably insincere in this. What they want is what Russia wants: i.e. to let the war go on, while dissociating themselves from it and using it as a process for getting their own ends. Unfortunately, the continuance of the war not only suits the hidden Communist aims, it is also essential to the British Empire. If we gave it up, Germany and Russia would be able to dictate any terms they like in the East of Europe, France would become a minor power, the British would have lost their prestige, and the Dominions would adopt a policy of *sauve qui peut* which would lead to the break-up of the Empire. If the war leads to a revolution under the influence of Russia involving the whole of central Europe, we shall at least have a breathing space, as the Red Armies will be occupied with regulating this vast new situation.

Then what are we fighting for? Personally, I think that we ought to be fighting a kind of defensive rearguard action against the development of absolutly chaotic and brutal conditions. It is absurd to fight to maintain the independence of small reactionary sovereign states. But it isn't absurd to fight in order to maintain our power, our prestige, and our democratic unity with France which would suffer a shattering blow if we accepted these peace terms. Then we can at least apply some sort of break when everything starts running downhill. E.g. We don't want to have another Poland like the old one, but we do want the rights of regions in a European Republic to be observed. In a way, I think the German-Soviet business holds out a hope for the future because a) it may lead to a breakdown of the present system of warring nationalisms, b) the larger the bloc becomes, the less important is the Prussian element in it; e.g. if it extends from Moscow to Berlin, the rights of the Czechs will have to be considered, c) Communism may now recover something of its former liberating socialist zeal. In short, the larger the movement becomes, the more likely it is to overthrow the tyrants who have started it. First Mussolini becomes a cypher, then Hitler, then perhaps Stalin.

In 1929-31, one saw very clearly for a short time the directions events were taking. Then, for some people, the conditions they were used to re-established themselves, and for ten years there were an England and France in a precarious balance. We now see again the plot. But there may be several years before it unfolds itself. . . .

Yesterday I lunched with Peter Watson and Cecil Beaton, [17] who Peter says is like me in some ways. I do actually see a certain resemblance because there is something ascetic about his appearance and character, in spite of his affectations. After lunch we went to see a portrait of him by Bérard. In the afternoon, I went to the Buhlers' and Tony Witherby came along and gave us advice about type-setting and type. The important thing is to have a rule to measure out the spacing. When we get one, I suppose I shall understand how it is done.

At 6 o'clock, Witherby, Peter, Diana W., Cyril and I had a long conference about the magazine he proposes to start. I pressed that there should be features on the subject of Culture and War, so that we should be able to keep a constant criticism of how broadcasting, publishing, music, art are going.

Earlier on, Cyril talked a bit about the war. He said that we were all wishful thinkers about Russia, that Stalin sympathized with Hitler as a "strong" man, and detested the British Empire and the line of British Cabinet Ministers from whom he has recovered so many states.

The blackout time gets a few minutes earlier each evening, so one notices more than ever the drawing in of the autumn evenings. Actually, the weather has been particularly fine lately. The streets glitter a biscuit yellow all day. The crowds waiting at the bus stops for the few buses give the town an air of festivity. The sand bags on the sidewalks, the strips of paper on the windows, the ballons in the air, are sufficiently new in the bright sunlight to be interesting and almost gay. . . .

When I drew the blinds, I felt the Autumn chill in my bones, and because of the decision I have taken which is really simply a recognition of existing facts, I had a sudden sense of the desolation of the world. Above all, the world should be home, it should be somewhere where everyone has his place, is surrounded by the simple machinery, the task, the house, the furniture, the companion, the river, the trees or the streets which assure him that he is loved. Everyone should be rooted. This is the simplest thing in life: it is the cocoon that surrounds childhood, it is the simple security of the flesh and the kiss and the fireplace and the setting sun which brings him home. The hands that destroy this homeliness whether in children or grown people are ripping the child in all of us that never leaves the womb away from the womb, and tearing the belly of the mother into ribbons. No one would want anything except to find his place in life, the center of his potentiality to love and be loved.

Yet if love is the essential thing in life, lovelessness is the fiend and the madness which enters certain bodies and tears the life surrounding them into shreds. The depredations of the loveless and homeless who seek power over their fellow beings can be seen everywhere today. The world suffers from the worst and least necessary of mental illnesses—homesickness. The papers are filled with photographs, and have been now for years, of those who have been driven out of their homes—the endless rustle of shuffling peasant feet through the dust all night along the road outside Malaga. The family with their possessions piled on a cart outside a burning Polish farmhouse. The widow searching amongst the ruins of her house for a souvenir. They are driven from the little hole which surrounded and comforted them into the elemental world of alien stones and light. Most homeless of all, little shreds of matter from distant countries that have nothing to do with them are driven through their flesh. The whole universe of death enters their bodies—a fragment of a bomb, a bullet.

After that in the world today there is the desolation of ideas. In times of war and revolution, the great comfort has always been that in place of home there is the house of ideas. One goes out into the street and finds that everyone is friendly, everyone is a brother or sister of everyone else because the family of the Homeland is threatened. The home of the idea, patriotism, revolutionary fervor, can knit people together into a spasmodic unity which is even greater than the happiest family life. But today, for hundreds of people, even that consolation is denied them. The greatest desolation in the world is produced by the confusion of ideas. Many no longer can fight for their country with any conviction, which is to fight for the house of the Past. And the house of the Future, Revolution, is so compromised that only the most ideological thinkers are able to want to fight for that either. Suddenly the world appears a desert. There is no woman, there are no children, there is no faith, there is no cause.

The moon shines above the London streets during the blackouts like an island in the sky. The streets become rivers of light. The houses become feathery, soft, undefined, aspiring, so that any part of this town might be the most beautiful city in the world, sleeping amongst silt and water. And the moon takes a farewell look at our civilization everywhere. I have seen it in Valencia, Barcelona, and Madrid, also. Only the houses were not plumed, feathery, soft there. The moon was brighter and they seemed made of white bone. . . .

I had lunch with [Eliot] a few days ago at the club. The stupid thing is that I can hardly remember anything of what we said. I remember that we had Port Salud cheese, which he chose. We each had a half of draft beer, so we were very abstemious. He smoked his French cigarettes. He was very gentle and courteous, as he always is, and more than that he talked with a great deal of freedom, was not at all the "great man." At lunch I said that it might be a good thing to start a new magazine now. He agreed heartily, but asked whether I thought we could get any subscribers. I said, not till January, I suppose. He asked me what I was doing, and I said, I think, writing my posthumous works, and that I wasn't taking any official job. He said, "I think it's very important that as many writers as possible should remain detached and not have any official position." I mentioned that I had sent in my name to the Ministry of Information and the War Office, but had had no reply. He had done ditto to the F[oreign] O[ffice] and had also had no reply.

He said he had designed a cover for his children's book about cats.[18] "I don't know whether it's altogether successful. I find that in drawing it seems purely a matter of chance whether I get the expression I want on a cat face or not. So I have to make a great many drawings, and hope that sooner or later I'll strike in the expression I want."

About writing, he said that it was very important that one should, at all costs, go on writing now. "It doesn't seem to me to matter very much whether one isn't able to do anything very good. The important thing is to keep going. Probably it's impossible to do excellent work while things are so disturbed."

I mentioned that I hadn't been able to work, so had started this journal. He said, "Yes, that's an excellent idea. Just writing every day is a way of keeping the engine running, and then something good may come out of it."

He talked a little about Joyce. "If he wrote anything now, it would have to be so entirely different from *Finnegans Wake* that one can easily imagine the necessary reorganization of his whole way of thinking would be too much for him." I said that perhaps he might write something simple, and added that one could imagine his thought being clear and simple, as, indeed, it is in parts of *F. W.*, but that it would be difficult to imagine him using a simpler vocabulary. Still more so abandoning his linguistic discoveries.

Eliot said that he did not care to listen to Beethoven so much just now. We both agreed on Bach and Glück for the war.

I said how necessary I felt it to be to be lucid in poetry when the world was so confused. Eliot said he thought the poetic drama might be a way of attaining lucidity, because, I suppose, it puts one outside oneself, whereas the poem tends today to be an introspective monologue. He praised *Trial of a Judge*, but said I couldn't have presented the same situation in that way today. I said I was attracted by but also sick of public events being dealt with in a public manner in plays. We agreed that the problem was to write about a smaller theme—perhaps family life—which had all the implications of what is going on in the world outside.

We talked about writing poetry. I tried to explain my difficulties. I write entirely from ear and from my own inner sense of what the poem should be. That is to say that from the first few lines which occur to me suddenly as a "gift" of inspiration, I work the rest out simply by writing and rewriting, so as to develop the logic of what I have to say as fully and clearly as possible. I dream that one might attain a great freedom in this way. But there are disadvantages in this way of writing which is "par excellence" the method of the "vers librist." In the first place, it concentrates entirely on expression, and is only poetry in so far as the thought happens to be poetry. Whereas if one chooses a form which is in itself poetic, like any of the well-known traditional forms, the traditional use of the form tends to-wards poetry, to which one conforms. In other words, accepted forms tend towards an objective realization of what form requires if it is to be successfully used, whereas my way tends towards subjective needs and standards. On the other hand, contemporary writing which fits into traditional standards does not really interest me. [Eliot] agreed with me about this, and he seemed also to agree that Auden's virtuosity in using accepted forms, while it certainly saves him from extremes of subjectivity and also, to some extent, from absurdity, has evaded the real problem—which is to discover new, recognized, generally acceptable forms suited to the requirements of today.

Another consequence of my way of writing is that I have no predisposition towards any particular medium. I have a prejudice in favour of poetry, a romantic feeling about the poet, a desire to achieve immortality, a desire to condense what I have to say in the shortest and most memorable phrase possible. . . . But really my only qualification as a writer is that I have something to say. That is, my situation [as an individual] human being seems to me interesting and potentially, if it is fully realized, to contain implications reaching out into the whole of contemporary life. Thus the view of some Communist writers that today one can only write about the workers and from their point of view seems to me not only nonsense, but also inhibitive and destructive to literature—at all events, until after the workers' revolution when, presumably, working class writers will write about workers. The important thing is to write about what one knows and realize it as fully as possible. If one lived in the depths of the country and felt that the only point in existence was to live in the town, the real dramatic center of one's position, if one were to realize it in writing, would be one's vision of the town which would be unreal, imposed on the reality of one's position in the country. To come to town and try to become the most conventional of urban writers would be to destroy one's imaginative gift. Yet that is the attitude of Communist critics towards bourgeois writers when they want to become workers. The fact is that the interest of the bourgeois writer who becomes a Communist is the penetrating insight he then gets into the life he already knows, which is now no longer isolated but implies the life of the workers beyond it. There are no negative situations in life—everything implies that which is complementary to it.

This is a digression, and I did not say all of it to [Eliot]. What I did state was my difficulty: that owing to my preoccupation with what I have to say rather than the means of saying it, I could, theoretically at all events, write in any medium. It is simply a question of expressing "the situation" in one form or another and then, by writing and rewriting, working out the logic of the form for myself. But the question is whether working everything out in this way one isn't working always back to the same center, expressing the subjective in subjective terms according to subjective standards. For example, if there were some accepted form of excellence recognized by the age—such as the heroic couplet in the 18th Century—one could judge one's performance by the standard of excellence in this.

[Eliot] said that an objective form might be the poetic drama, because here one had to meet one's audience half-way and adopt to some extent their standards. I agreed, but this of course raised the question of whether the poetic drama was a suitable form for the drama today. Unless this is so, poetic dramas published as books are just a waste of good poetry—if they are poetic. [Eliot] also said that he wasn't sure whether he didn't feel as I did about writing poetry. I asked him whether he didn't feel that perhaps the trick of his poetry wasn't to make the reader identify himself with Tom Eliot and enter into his subjective mood. Then how could one be sure that at a later time when the personal situations of [his] poetry are no longer such as people can easily enter into that his poetry won't be seen from the outside—much as we see the work of the 'Eighties, for example. He agreed that this was a problem.

I was very glad to have put my difficulty in writing verse before him, and to find that he understood it. That is all I remember of our conversation, though I dare say we speculated about the war.

October 1st

Wrote this diary last night and read about half of Isaiah Berlin's book on Marx.[19]

October 19th

So it seems that I have made no entry in my diary for eighteen days, and the time is approaching when there will be such a congestion of material that I will not know where to start and will give up the diary altogether. Here I am on the track of one of the main forces which inhibit writers from getting on with their work—the accumulation of unfulfilled tasks and projects and ideas, which finally so confuse one that one prefers forgetting one's inspiration and waiting for something new to dealing with this excess of material.

Let me sort things out a bit, make a list of my ideas, and try to find some solution to the problem of having a superfluity of subjects. What have I done during the past few weeks? What are the ideas which I have had in mind all the time but which seemed to difficult to undertake? Just as if one was being dragged round in a whirlpool in the center of which there was an iron post to catch hold of, the difficulty of catching hold of it might be so great that finally one would become grateful to the very speed and rush of the waters which pulled one away and so spared one from making an effort!

That eighteen days can become lost, a mere torrent of movement and distraction and running round! What I've had at the back of my mind all the time is that I ought to write an account of my weekend at the Woolves, which I still see as a kind of raft where I was for a few days. Then after that there were five days at Humphrey's flat, most of which I spent in typing out my novel, although I still haven't finished doing that. Then there was the weekend at Isaiah Berlin's at Oxford. Since then, I have been in London staying first at Humphrey's then at the Buhlers', where Bobby and I spent most of our time printing. During all this time I have seen many people, made many arrangements, and the last part of it has been overshadowed by something which I cannot write about, and which really had the effect of making me lose all desire to be married or not married, or to live at any particular place, because it was so close and yet so much worse than anything that has happened to me personally.

It wasn't only this diary I wanted to write, but also my novel and a long Eclogue, which I started at Isaiah's. Perhaps now this will be possible. I have notes in a brown book for about a dozen poems I want to get on with. Yet nothing drives poetry so much out of one's head as big projects, like a novel or anything sustained. Perhaps one day I shall give up the idea of writing any books altogether, and just write poems. Also, note that I have two short stories in mind, one called "Amy," the other an account of a walk in the churchyard near here. In addition to this, there is the work connected with *Horizon*, which I enjoy. There are also one or two things that I wanted to write about in this Journal, apart from meeting with people. One is solitude. The other is the attitude of writers to contemporary life in an amoral age. Also, I've decided to do an account of the background of Christopher's Berlin novels.

When I think of these things, I am tempted to get up and go out for a walk. If I decide to do one of them I am only drawing my own attention to the fact that I am not doing the other. Happiness would lie in doing them all, and having a full life as well. I'll try to do them all. The result may be a sense of failure, but the consolation will be that at the end of a few months I find I have after all done something. Perhaps I should try to evolve a shorter way of writing things in this journal, simply in order to spare myself a certain amount of physical labour.

October 20th

After I had written the above, I went across to the Buhlers', intending to print. However, Philip Hope Wallace was there, and instead of working, we talked. He was extremely depressed, said that since he had no desire to write a great book or paint a great picture, there was nothing for him to live for, except to see his standard of living slowly decline and the world around him grow more unpleasant. He said that there was no possibility of improvement in the world unless there was a complete revolution of the social and economic system, but that this would never take place under the old dodderers who govern us. He also said that there was nothing that he himself would hate more than such a change, if it came about. This talk lowered our morale considerably, and Bobby turned on him and said that he got a great deal of pleasure out of sneering at the world, and also that his misery was to some extent enjoyable. I got impatient too and said that however bad things were, the very fact that one survived and was not destroyed by them was a source of happiness; what one must learn was at once to go on caring and yet be detached—to care and not to care.

We dined at a little restaurant near here. After dinner, Veronica and Jacqueline came round, and we talked again. I lunched yesterday at Mary Smith's, and apart from writing this journal, the rest of the day was spent on *Horizon*.

It must now be three weeks since my weekend at the Woolves. They live in a very pleasant house at Rodmell near Lewes. The view from the garden looks across to the downs near Newhaven. There is a plain between the garden and the downs where the railway runs to Newhaven. The other side of the house is the village, so that on one side the country is open and spacious; on the other, it is a closed-in valley. I like this effect very much. The Woolves have a large pond with water lilies and a great many gold fish in their garden.

I arrived in time for tea. After tea, we went out onto the lawn and played a game of bowls. I had beginner's luck, and I think won the first game, though I never succeeded so well afterwards. Virginia and I walked about the garden talking about writing, which she said she wanted to discuss with other writers. She was pleased that I kept a journal because she said she found it was the only thing she could do, too. She thought that every day an occasion arises in which one sees things in an entirely new and different way, that these moments of transformation are one's grasp on reality. This is the experience which she tries to catch hold of in her journal.

She talked also about the danger of creating a literary personality for oneself. Her dislike of self-importance links up with her dislike of the egotism of successful men. She said that the mistake of ambitious women was to try to compete with men on their own ground, to become masculine. Women had a life of their own which they could develop without being diminished by men.

I shan't go on with this—I have lost the thread. So I'll just note down the rest of the weekend, together with a few other events of the past days. On the Sunday, we went for a walk on the Downs in the afternoon and Leonard and I discussed politics. Duncan Grant,[20] Angelica, and a girl friend came to tea, after which we played bowls again. . . .

October 21st

Yesterday morning I tried to work writing the journal, but I found it very much against the grain. Tony was here doing secretarial work for *Horizon* and we quarrelled about various stupid things, such as whether or not to address letters c/o *New Writing*.

Lunched at Mary Smith's and left directly afterwards. Came home and wrote to Christopher Isherwood,[21] then went to Buhler's. He was setting up type in the chase, which I am not much use at, so I hung about with nothing to do. Met Cyril at 7.15 at the Cumberland Hotel. We compared the first contributions we had received. . . . Dined with Humphrey and Lolly. I was depressed by the atmosphere of nurse and Bertha in the house. Lolly had been visited by Inez in the afternoon. This depressed me too for some reason, and has revived a lot of my obsession with that affair. . . .

October 22nd

We came to Lavenham. Bobby, Eve, Peter and I left by car at 11 and arrived here for a latish lunch. In the afternoon, we picked mushrooms in the fields. In the evening I played some gramophone records, Beethoven's op. 127 Quartet and the last movement of op. 132. This last movement seems to me the most mysterious and religious of all Beethoven's ideas. It has a line which exists amongst the arid, harsh surrounding orchestration like a view of a distant, blue range of mountains beyond a rolling desert. At times the rocks shut out this refreshing vision, but it always exists beyond them, and at moments one is immersed completely in it, until finally as one at last turns away it is repeated with fervent ecstasy. Wonderful the passage at the end where one thinks the movement is finished, and it is repeated very quickly in between final chords so that when the chords do close there is a suggestion of it again, a suggestion that this pure, limpid refreshment goes on forever.

October 23

I had bad dreams. In one I dreamt that I went into a house with someone who in some way resembled M. In the passage there were two recesses, one for Ashes, the other concealed a button. Knowing that the result would be fatal, I pressed the button. A man came forward with a revolver, intending to shoot us. I trembled violently, but I thought, "Now we have found you out. Now we know where we are, at all events."

A second dream. I was in a room facing a street with Lolly, who was ill but up and working at her architecture. Then I saw Helen cross the street outside in order to buy something which would please us, tickets for the theater perhaps. But she was going away very hurriedly, and as she crossed the street, it looked as though she might be run over. Lolly realized this too, and ran out of the house after Helen. I felt the most acute anxiety and fear that first something was going to happen. I felt very guilty and started thinking of excuses, such as that Lolly had been told to lead a normal life. Meanwhile, I saw that Helen had disappeared, and that Lolly, in running after her, was almost run over. She was running wildly after Helen, and just then a police van drove up; the policemen got out and started attacking her with truncheons. Realizing that she was ill, this moment was so terrible for me that I remember nothing of what happened in the next few seconds. Then I went out onto the street and an open car drove up with Lolly, almost dead, Helen and Inez in the back seat. Inez got out of the car, threw her arms round me and said, "I have come back." I felt relieved, and at the same time that anything like that was too late now.

October 24th

Peter, the Buhlers, Humphrey and I spent yesterday at Lavenham. In the afternoon we went for a bike ride. Bobby was very gay, pretending to bike in various different ways, whistling, sticking his hands in his pockets. The country extremely beautiful, rich as though laid on with a trowel. I enjoyed the ride very much. Peter and I came home in the evening in a blacked-out, blue-lit train. We now live in a blue period Picasso.

October 25th

Yesterday I worked hard all day. In the morning wrote some of my novel and a poem for Humphrey. Also wrote to Wystan, Wells, Kathleen and William about *Horizon*. At 5 o'clock, went to the Buhlers' and set up type. Eve pregnant. Bobby not very well and rather preoccupied with his health, I thought. I was slightly annoyed with him and Tony Witherby for not getting on with the job. This is silly. Had a drink with Cyril to discuss more about *Horizon*, particularly J. B. Priestley's letter offering us the serial rights of his play.[22] Cyril told me that Jeannie went out at 7 o'clock on Sunday night to see some friends round the corner, intending to return in a few minutes for dinner. While there, she fell into a deep sleep, in the middle of drinking only one glass of whiskey. Her host undressed her and put her to bed and she did not wake until 10 o'clock the next morning. He told me that since then she has been sleeping most of the day. The war seems to have the effect of making people who are weak in some way crack up. "It pushes people over the edge whose health or sex or sanity is uncertain," said Cyril. I smiled and said, "In my case I lose on sex."

October 26th

Wrote all the morning, lunched with Grigson[23] at the Café Royal. As soon as he saw me, he said, "I say, is Cyril seriously going to call his magazine *Horizon*?" "I think so," I said, rather damped. "Anyhow, what's your objection?" "Well, magazines called *Horizon* never last for more than two numbers," he said. "What other magazines have been called *Horizon*?" "I don't know, but it's a metaphor and a pretty trite one. It suggests flatness, the flatness of the dead." "Well, it's been quite well-received by everyone we've told about it." "Oh," said Grigson, "it wasn't so well received last night at a dinner party at Henley. Betjeman and Piper were there. In fact, to be perfectly frank, there was quite a lot of laughter about *Horizon*." "Well," I said, "as a matter of fact, I thought of *Horizon*." This mollified him somewhat. Then he said, "By the way, who is doing the publishing and the distributing?" "Witherby's," I said. "Witherby's?" he repeated, incredulously. "Yes." "How delightful, how charming. It's such an original idea that it really has quite an appeal." He looked graver and added, "Of course, there are disadvantages in publishing in London. It will cost you at least 15% more, I should say." I explained that Witherby was a friend of ours. He was then very helpful and said he would let me have all his material for the now defunct *New Verse*. He also gave me various hints about the importance of set-up and paragraphs in a magazine. I am very grateful for these and shall remember them. However, he had soon started again on a new tack. "You may not believe it," he said, looking slightly embarrassed, "but I've always put you on a bit of a pedestal. So I was very disappointed at a remark by you in *The New Statesman* which I thought beneath you, the other day."[24]

Afterwards we joined Cyril and went through the *Horizon* discussion again. Later Cyril said to me, "We bow our heads. We accept Grigson's sneers, and thank him for them. But we might have pointed out that if *Horizon* is a dead title, *New Verse* is dead and done for. And if a metaphor is flat, nothing is so positively sickening in a title as the adjective "New."

After lunch, we had an editorial meeting.

Then I went to the Buhlers' after tea. A little of the really shining quality has gone from them, and they have worries too. Eve is pregnant, and Bobby is anxious about his own health also.

In the evening, dined with Jack Barker at Chop Suey. After dinner we had coffee at the Café Royal. We sat next to a drunken doctor, and party, from Leeds. The doctor's conversation was like the medicos in *Ulysses* and I enjoyed it very much.

We went upstairs and talked to Cyril, Joan Rayner and her sister and then I went home.

Advantages of living alone. Increase of energy and creativeness because I can indulge without qualms of conscience in the brutal selfishness of being a writer.

When I am living with someone, I am always reproaching myself for not paying her enough attention. This means that all the time I feel under a certain [con]straint. It also means that I attach far too much importance to other people's whims and moods which make me feel guilty of inconsiderateness. I feel that pleasures which people might, in fact, easily sacrifice, are mysteriously important, and this makes any decision, like living in the country or demanding that my wife should stop having an "affair" etc., very difficult. In fact altogether there is a lack of confidence in any behavior within a possessive relationship. The effect of this is not to lessen but rather increase the egotism which I am trying to repress in myself.

It is really rather disturbing to write this. I do not even entirely understand what I am trying to explain yet. But what it comes to is that when someone I am with whom I am accustomed to think of as happy is unhappy, I experience a feeling of deep apprehension, a sense that nothing is ever going to be better now, because I have discovered that everything is wrong. At the same time, a corresponding distress of my own is revealed by my companion's unhappiness, and soon I feel that it is I who am making her unhappy. In certain cases, I even manage to persuade her that this is so.

I can only imagine that these feelings have something to do with my mother being an invalid. When we were children, our mother was often well and even gay. But nevertheless, the fundamental fact about her was that she was ill—or so we were told. The happiness of a summer day was fragile—a raised voice, a quarrel with my brothers or sister would break it, and then the headaches would begin. "You have given Mummy a headache," etc. I never trust anyone I am with not suddenly to break down and reveal some fundamental physical or mental disability.

But it is not only unhappiness that distresses me deeply, but also tiredness, laziness, and other weaknesses in people. I don't mention this, but I freeze with horror. When I was sixteen and used to go home in the tube from my grandmother's house on Sunday evenings, a thing that irritated me almost beyond bearing was if my sister or her companion, who were with me, yawned. The fact was that I was very tired myself, but it was impossible for me to relax even so far as to yawn, and the fact that there were people who yawned, unthinkingly, not accepting the necessity I saw of never revealing that one was tired, maddened me.

I know I am giving myself away far more than if I owned, for example, that I had committed a murder. The real crimes in post-war society are sexual incompetence and Puritan traits of character. If one is guilty of these, none of the punishments of domestic life is bad enough. One's wife and friends soon find out and proceed to adopt a really merciless attitude in which they are completely justified.

However, now that I am alone, there is no reason why I should not be frank. It is as though a special set of rules applies to my own life which do not apply to other people. These rules were put into my head by my father, whether he was conscious or not of it. He was furiously ambitious for at least two of his sons, and particularly for me. I hated his kind of journalistic ambitiousness, but I was only able to wriggle out of it by substituting an even more difficult ambition of my own. Instead of being a fake great man, I wanted to be a real great writer. I have resisted my own ambition by sabotaging it for years. But the only relief for me now is to give way to the desire to write endlessly. What is so difficult to understand is that there are people who are not ambitious, either in a publicist or in a truer sense; they just enjoy themselves and are content to be ignored. It does not seem fair. I learned from my father that it was silly to want to be Lloyd George, but how can I learn that it is silly to want to be Beethoven or Shakespeare? I shall have to be all I can be in order to learn this.

One day I might meet some adult person who understood and forgave what I feel. Meanwhile, though, it's better to be alone. Then my moods are my own, and they don't upset anyone else, and I can give way to my intolerable ambition. I still haven't explained this right.

October 27th

Yesterday was another day of hard work. I finished the poem for H. Lunched at Mary Smith's. George Barker called at 5.30, and we went along to the Buhlers'. Bobby was in a very irritable mood because someone he did not want to see was coming to supper. But we put this person off and I took him out and we had a bottle of wine. Then we went to the Café Royal where we met Michael [Spender].

10.30 p.m. Today has been a gray day. I worked in the morning, I suppose, though I hardly seem to remember what I did. At lunch there was O. B.; rather silly, I thought, and a feminine way of tilting his head up at you as though under a cloche hat, and looking through half-closed eyelids. He had a friend dressed entirely in corduroy. I saw Cyril before lunch and felt rather uneasy with him. Before tea I went to the *New Statesman* and got some books to review.[25] Then I went to Humphrey and Lolly's for tea. Lolly was looking very pale, but was as gentle and nice as she always is. I had an absurd panic that I was going to say the wrong thing, and I kept on talking about people being ill. A letter from Sally Graves was there, saying I had better accept the situation about Inez, and go on with the divorce. This, just because it was about her, upset me, as it did when I heard she had visited Lolly the other day. I think it probably would be best to go on with the divorce, but a) I have other things to spend the money on now, b) If she asked me not to do it, I am sure I would give way, even now. The fact is that I don't believe any longer that I shall marry or even love anyone else. Those sort of feelings don't seem to have any future for me. . . . I have a sense of loss, and in spite of myself, I still feel cruel and vindictive; one of the things I most resent about the whole business is that it produces in me many feelings that I am ashamed of. Well, I'll try writing a bit of my novel.

Idea for a story about Ralph Bates in Madrid.[26]

November 16th

I have given up the idea of writing events from day to day here. That is not my way. It is best to write reminiscences and meditations and fragmentary [soon]-lost illuminations which occur to one just before one is going to sleep, or on a walk or in the bathroom, when a whole sequence of things is as clear and yet featureless as a face remembered in a dream.

When I was a child I used to try thinking of something perfectly familiar, like my mother's face or a postage stamp. I could imagine it so clearly that it seemed even livelier than the real image. But I could only think of it as a whole impression. When I tried to imagine the features separately or to relate the proportions to each other, I realized that I could never draw them from my mental image, which immediately began to lose conviction and faded.

The very rigid mental image of a sequence of words, just as one is taking one's socks off to go to bed, is like a view of mountains from an airplane. They lie there making a single, complex but comprehensible shape, with folds in them. But one hoards the sense of distance for fear of being lost if one were down there amongst the verbs and other difficult parts of speech.

But that isn't the whole problem. It's not just the lack of courage and patience that one fears, but that the descent into language actually puts one wrong. The words suggest their own sequences, partly dictated by the rules of language, partly by cliché and everything one reads, partly by habits of thought which one has formed. One repeats the same mistakes, one finds that instead of bringing down to earth the singular and floating vision, one is just writing the same thing as one wrote before.

How I fear that I will fall again into the grooves of words which instead of expressing what I see, drag me along their lines away from it! I leave long gaps between my poems in the hope that the last will not influence the next one, and perhaps I will create [finally] the real image of what in a moment I thought and saw.

Yet it's not just a matter of willing and working at it. It's a matter of letting oneself go. Somewhere in one there's a fountain of words that are wanting to say the thing I can say, only directly I set myself to will them out of me, the fears, ambitions, habits of thought, prejudices, demands of style form a barrier between me and what is perfectly clear, if only I could reach it. On this side of the barrier where I am seated at my desk, I can only produce the faint imitation of something on the other side of my will.

It's a matter of patiently waiting till the moment comes, and then not disturbing it; of listening and praying, not punishing oneself with threats. How is it that I am innocent when I punish myself so unceasingly?

If I didn't punish myself, the true strength of my innocence would flower without effort in my undemanding love for people and my ease of words.

I have lost it. I am conscious of the bone of my forehead.

Jack, I think of you, Jack Tar, sailor on the slippery boards and with muscles strained against the rope and surge of wars.

Stammering in your speech, fragments of sky in your eyes, frowning in your face at the difficulty of the sun.

Trim-waisted, cliff-chested, peasant-handed, with a navel chiseled in an abdomen of stone.

Hair coiled to rings by spray kisses; you approached

With palms extended and a wide smile,

Me, who am contorted in my bowels with the sorrows of a town.

And kissing the shell of my ear, you held me in the sea's grip,

And broke my bones and the walls of my loneliness, and pounded to laughter my ribs,

And threw upon the guilt of my shore the sun and the salt and the archaic god's gift.

Rewrite this.

Two days ago, I went out with my sister to a cocktail party given by a Catholic lady doctor.

Notes to Appendix

¹ Spender met Isaiah Berlin, the philosopher of history, at Oxford. *World Within World* is dedicated to Berlin.

² Ernst Toller. Spender writes in *WWW*, "Shortly before the war, the German poet Ernst Toller came to see me. He had some scheme which he wanted to discuss, about an appeal through high functionaries to the conscience of the world on behalf of the Spanish Republicans. . . . Toller invited Inez and me to dine with him one night at the Gargoyle Club. He had ideas of himself as a gallant, so all through dinner he was markedly attentive to Inez. Indeed there was something fascinating about him with his large brown eyes like a doe's, and his pale skin like an American Indian's. At the end of the dinner, Toller, rather surprisingly, fished a silver brooch out of his pocket and presented it to Inez.

"A few days later Toller hanged himself. I read this in the newspapers and was deeply shocked. When I told Inez, her face became distorted with anger as I had never seen it before, for she did not as a rule dramatize things. She turned on me furiously: 'You understand why he committed suicide. You *would* know someone capable of doing such a thing. That's what I can't bear about you,' and she threw the brooch which Toller had given her, across the room" (pp. 258-59).

³ Cyril Connolly, who edited *Horizon* from 1940 until it ceased publication in 1949, and and his American wife Jean.

⁴ Arthur Greenwood, Minister without portfolio, 1940-42; Sir Archibald Sinclair, Leader of the Liberal Party, Secretary of State for Air, 1940-45.

⁵ This paragraph has an X drawn through it in the original.

⁶ Staatliches Bauhaus school of design, founded by Walter Gropius; members of the group attempted to end the schism between crafts and architecture.

⁷ Ernst Robert Curtius.

[8] "The Solitary Reaper."

[9] André Maurois, *Byron* (Paris: Bernard Grasset, 1930).

[10] "The Second Coming."

[11] Dylan Thomas, *The Map of Love* (London: J.M. Dent and Sons, 1939).

[12] "Unfortunately I can't find any connections in Berlin for you."

[13] *The Backward Son* (London: The Hogarth Press, 1940).

[14] Soon, Barker left England for a university post in Japan; a year later he went to the United States.

[15] *Horizon.*

[16] A treaty signed in Moscow on September 18, 1939, established friendly relations between Germany and Russia. The two countries partitioned Poland, and the Soviets pledged Germany economic support.

[17] The photographer Cecil Beaton worked as a wartime photographer for the Ministry of Information, covering fighting in Africa and the Far East.

[18] Eliot's *Old Possum's Book of Practical Cats* (London: Faber and Faber, 1939) had a yellow dustwrapper which contained designs by Eliot.

[19] Berlin's *Karl Marx: His Life and Environment* (London: Oxford University Press, 1939) dismissed the idea of an objective march of history and the belief that all values are conditioned by the place men occupy on the "moving stair of time."

[20] Duncan Grant was a Scottish painter and decorative artist, influenced by Cézanne. Angelica was the daughter of Clive and Vanessa Bell, and Virginia Woolf's niece.

[21] This letter is lost.

[22] Probably Priestley's *Johnson Over Jordan*, which appeared in 1939.

[23] Geoffrey Grigson was the founder and editor of *New Verse*. His review of a number of new volumes of verse appears in the first number of *Horizon*.

[24] Probably a reference to Spender's review of some new translations of Greek verse, "The Greeks in the Black-Out," which appeared in the October 14 issue of *The New Statesman and Nation*.

[25] In the November 11 issue of *The New Statesman and Nation*, Spender reviewed *On the Boiler* by Yeats, and *The Arrow: W. B. Yeats Commemoration Number*.

[26] Ralph Bates, the novelist, was elected leader of the English Delegation to the International Congress in Spain in 1937.

Spender, Isherwood, and the Thirties
A Selected Bibliography

Works by Stephen Spender, 1928-1939

Nine Experiments. London: privately printed, 1928.
Twenty Poems. Oxford: Basil Blackwell, 1930.
Poems. London: Faber and Faber, 1933.
Vienna. London: Faber and Faber, 1934.
The Destructive Element. London: Jonathan Cape, 1935.
The Burning Cactus. London: Faber and Faber, 1936.
Forward from Liberalism. London: Victor Gollancz Ltd., 1937.
Trial of a Judge. London: Faber and Faber, 1938.
The New Realism. London: The Hogarth Press, 1939.
The Still Centre. London: Faber and Faber, 1939.

Works by Christopher Isherwood, 1928-1939

All the Conspirators. London: Jonathan Cape, 1928.
The Memorial. London: The Hogarth Press, 1932.
Mr. Norris Changes Trains. London: The Hogarth Press, 1935.
The Dog Beneath the Skin. With W. H. Auden. London: Faber and Faber, 1935.
The Ascent of F6. With W. H. Auden. London: Faber and Faber, 1936.
Sally Bowles. London: The Hogarth Press, 1937.
On the Frontier. With W. H. Auden. London: Faber and Faber, 1938.
Lions and Shadows. London: The Hogarth Press, 1938.
Goodbye to Berlin. London: The Hogarth Press, 1939.
Journey to a War. With W. H. Auden. London: Faber and Faber, 1939.

Secondary Sources

Auden, W. H. *Collected Poems.* Edited by Edward Mendelson. New York: Random House, 1976.

———. *The English Auden: Poems, Essays and Dramatic Writings, 1927-1939.* Edited by Edward Mendelson. New York: Random House, 1977.

Bantock, G. H. "The Novels of Christopher Isherwood," in *The Novelist as Thinker.* Edited by B. Rajan. London: D. Dobson, 1947.

Bloomfield, B. C. *W. H. Auden: A Bibliography, the Early Years through 1955.* Charlottesville: The University of Virginia, 1964.

Buell, Frederick. *W. H. Auden as a Social Poet.* Ithaca, New York: Cornell University Press, 1973.

Crossman, Richard, ed. *The God that Failed.* New York: Harper, 1949.

Evans, Benjamin Ifor. *English Literature Between the Wars.* London: Methuen and Company, 1949.

Finney, Brian. *Christopher Isherwood: A Critical Biography.* New York: Oxford University Press, 1979.

Glicksberg, Charles. "Poetry and Marxism: Three English Poets Take their Stand." *University of Toronto Quarterly,* 3 (April, 1937), pp. 309-325.

Heibrun, Carolyn G. *Christopher Isherwood.* New York: Columbia University Press, 1970.

Hoskins, Katherine B. *Today the Struggle: Literature and Politics in England During the Spanish Civil War.* Austin: University of Texas Press, 1969.

Hynes, Samuel. *The Auden Generation: Literature and Politics in England in the 1930's.* New York: The Viking Press, 1976.

Isherwood, Christopher. *Christopher and His Kind.* London: Methuen, 1977.

King, Francis. *Christopher Isherwood.* London: Longman Group, 1976.

Kulkarni, H. B. *Stephen Spender: Poet in Crisis.* Glasgow: Blackie and Son, 1970.

———. *Stephen Spender: Works and Criticism, an Annotated Bibliography.* New York: Garland Publishing, 1976.

Lehmann, John. *The Whispering Gallery: Autobiography.* London: Longman, 1955.

Lewis, C. Day. *Collected Poems of C. Day Lewis*. London: Cape & Hogarth, 1954.

MacNeice, Louis. *The Collected Poems of Louis MacNeice*. Edited by E. R. Dodds. New York: Oxford University Press, 1967.

———. *The Strings are False: An Unfinished Autobiography*. New York: Oxford University Press, 1966.

Maxwell, D. E. S. *Poets of the Thirties*. London: Routledge & Kegan Paul, 1969.

Muggeridge, Malcolm. *The Thirties*. London: Hamish Hamilton, 1940.

Muste, John M. *Say that We Saw Spain Die: Literary Consequences of the Spanish Civil War*. Seattle: University of Washington Press, 1966.

Orwell, George. "Inside the Whale," in *Inside the Whale and Other Essays*. London: Victor Gollancz, 1940.

Replogle, Justin. "The Auden Group." *Wisconsin Studies in Contemporary Literature*, 5 (Summer, 1964), pp. 133-50.

———. "The Gang Myth in Auden's Early Poetry." *Journal of English and Germanic Philology*, 61 (1962), pp. 481-95.

Roberts, Michael, ed. *The Faber Book of Modern Verse*. London: Faber and Faber, 1936.

———. *New Country*. London: The Hogarth Press, 1933.

———. *New Signatures*. London: The Hogarth Press, 1932.

Piazza, Paul. *Christopher Isherwood: Myth and Anti-Myth*. New York: Columbia University Press, 1978.

Sellers, W. H. "Spender and Vienna." *Humanities Association Bulletin*, 18 (Spring, 1967), pp. 59-68.

Skelton, Robin, ed. *Poetry of the Thirties*. Harmondsworth, Middlesex: Penguin Books, 1971.

Smith, Elton Edward. *The Angry Young Men of the Thirties*. Carbondale, Illinois: Southern Illinois University Press, 1975.

Spears, Monroe K. *The Poetry of W. H. Auden: The Disenchanted Island*. New York: Oxford University Press, 1963.

Spender, Stephen, ed. *W. H. Auden: A Tribute*. New York: Macmillan, 1975.

———. *World Within World*. London: Hamish Hamilton, 1951.

Stanford, Derek. *Stephen Spender, Louis MacNeice, and Cecil Day Lewis: A Critical Essay*. Grand Rapids: Erdmans, 1969.

Stansky, Peter and William Abrahams. *Journey to the Frontier: Julian Bell and John Cornford—their Lives and the 1930's*. London: Constable, 1966.

Symons, Julian. *The Thirties: A Dream Revolved.* London: The Cresset Press, 1960.

Thomas, David P. *"Goodbye to Berlin:* Refocusing Isherwood's Camera." *Contemporary Literature,* 13 (winter, 1972), pp. 44-52.

Thomas, Hugh. *The Spanish Civil War.* Harmondsworth, Middlesex: Penguin Books, 1963.

Tolly, A. Trevor. *The Early Published Poems of Stephen Spender: A Chronology.* Ottawa: Carleton University, 1967.

———. *The Poetry of the Thirties.* New York: St. Martin's Press, 1976.

Weatherhead, A. Kingsley. *Stephen Spender and the Thirties.* Lewisburg: Bucknell University Press, 1975.

Weintraub, Stanley. *The Last Great Cause: The Intellectuals and the Spanish Civil War.* London: Allen, 1968.

Westby, Selmer and Clayton M. Brown. *Christopher Isherwood: A Bibliography, 1923-1967.* Los Angeles: California State College at Los Angeles Foundation, 1968.

Wilde, Alan. *Christopher Isherwood.* New York: Twayne Publishers, Inc., 1971.

Wood, Neal. *Communism and British Intellectuals.* London: Gollancz, 1959.

Woolf, Leonard. *Downhill All the Way: An Autobiography of the Years 1919-1939.* New York: Harcourt, Brace, and World, 1967.

Index

H., Karl, 51
Halsband, Robert, 17, 19n
Hamilton, Gerald, 21, 47, 59, 90n, 133
Hamsun, Knut (*Pan*), 53, 84n
Hansen, Erwin, 115, 137n
Hardy, Thomas, 150
Harman, Wolfgang, 51, 170–3
Heard, Gerald, 21, 62, 63, 85n, 106, 117, 118, 126, 135n
Heinz, 22, 47, 51, 54, 57, 59, 63, 64, 67, 68, 72, 74, 76–80, 87n, 88n, 90n, 102, 105–9, 117, 118, 120–2, 125, 127, 128, 130, 136n, 137n
Hellmut, 10, 11, 22, 43, 50–6, 59–61, 66, 69, 85n, 87n, 113, 141, 143–59
Hemingway, Ernest, 29, 51
Death in the Afternoon, 84n
Hicks, Seymour, 161
Hindenberg, Paul von, 59
Hitler, Adolf, 46, 59, 85n, 95, 98, 120, 132, 163, 164, 166, 171, 174, 181, 184, 188, 190, 191
Hogarth Press, 22, 24, 40n, 43, 46, 69, 73, 86–8n, 132
Hölderlin, Friedrich, 47, 74, 75, 78, 80, 90n, 113, 136n, 184
Homer, 116
Horizon, 141, 197–9, 201, 202, 207n, 208n
Horst, 171, 172
Hound and Horn, 89n
Hours Press, 86n
Hugo's Spanish in Three Months, 110, 136n
Huxley, Aldous, 16
Eyeless in Gaza, 120, 138n
Hyndman, Tony, 22, 45–7, 62, 63, 65–8, 70–2, 74, 75, 77, 78, 81, 86n, 91n, 95, 102, 103, 108, 112, 113, 115, 116, 118–21, 124, 126, 127, 129, 130, 136n, 140n, 162, 199

Hynes, Samuel, (*The Auden Generation*), 13, 14, 18, 43, 83n, 84n

Incitement to Disaffection Bill ("Sedition Bill"), 68, 87n
Isherwood, Christopher
All the Conspirators, 29
Ascent of F6, The (with Auden), 16, 21, 95, 102, 118, 121, 123, 124, 136n, 137n, 139n
Berlin Stories, 85n
Christopher and His Kind, 14, 18, 21, 22, 39n, 44, 45, 83–5n, 88n, 95, 103, 136n
Dog Beneath the Skin, The (*Where Is Francis?*; with Auden), 15, 21, 46, 75, 79, 89n, 91n, 111, 119, 122
Down There On a Visit, 23, 137n
Goodbye to Berlin, 14, 16, 23, 24, 40n, 83n, 137n
Journey to a War (with Auden), 31, 103
Lions and Shadows, 21n, 22, 24, 30, 39n, 102
Little Friend, 46, 66, 69, 87n
Lost, The, 46, 69, 87n, 88n
Memorial, The, 15, 22, 38, 40n, 43, 51, 86n, 88n
Mr. Norris Changes Trains, 14, 15, 21, 24, 46, 69, 87–9n
"Nowaks, The," 137n
On the Frontier (with Auden), 102

Jaqueline, 198
James, Henry, 45–7, 52, 62, 70, 86n, 98, 99
Letters, 84n
Jobst, 172, 173
Johnson, Basil, 188
Joyce, James, 29, 139n, 194
Finnegans Wake, 194
Ulysses, 202

Kafka, Franz, 87n
Kathleen, 189, 201
Keats, John, 29

217

218

Printed October 1980 in Santa Barbara & Ann Arbor for the Black
Sparrow Press by Mackintosh and Young & Edwards Brothers Inc.
Cover portrait of Stephen Spender by Wyndham Lewis. Design by
Barbara Martin. This edition is published in paper wrappers; there are
1000 cloth trade copies; 200 numbered hardcover copies are signed by
Stephen Spender; & 50 special copies have been handbound in boards
& slipcased by Earle Gray & are numbered & signed by Stephen
Spender & Lee Bartlett.

107

STEPHEN SPENDER was born in 1909, the second son of a Liberal journalist. He was educated at University College School, London, and University College, Oxford, where his friends included those writers with whom his name was to be linked as the Thirties Generation: Auden, Day Lewis, MacNeice, Isherwood, and Upward. In 1928 he printed his and Auden's first books of poems on his own hand press. His book, *Poems*, was accepted by T. S. Eliot for Faber and Faber and it appeared in 1933.

He went to Spain during the Spanish Civil War and worked as a propagandist for the Republicans. With Cyril Connolly he founded *Horizon* in 1939 and co-edited it until 1942 when he joined the National Fire Service in London. At the end of the Second World War, under the auspices of the Foreign Office, he traveled in Germany and France. With Irving Kristol he founded *Encounter* in 1953 and was its co-editor until 1965.

Since the late 1940s he has spent much time in the United States where he has been Visiting Professor at many universities; and in 1965-6 he was Consultant in Poetry at the Library of Congress. In England, he was Professor of English at University College, London, from 1968 to 1973. He has also traveled widely in Europe.

Stephen Spender published his *Collected Poems* in 1955 and has since published a further collection, *The Generous Days* (1971). His autobiography, *World Within World*, appeared in 1951. He has also published one play, *Trial of a Judge* (1938), a novel, *The Backward Son* (1940), and several books of criticism including *The Destructive Element* (1935) and *The Struggle of the Modern* (1963). His other prose books include *The Year of the Young Rebels* (1969) and *Love-Hate Relations* (1974). Among those writers whose work he has translated are Rilke, Büchner, Lorca, and Schiller.

LEE BARTLETT was born in Berkeley, California, in 1950. He holds B.A. and Ph.D. degrees from the University of California, has taught at the University of Bordeaux and the University of California at Davis, and is currently an Assistant Professor of English at Pikeville College in Kentucky. His poems, translations, and reviews have appeared in a number of journals, including the *California Quarterly, London Magazine*, the *New York Quarterly*, and the *San Francisco Review of Books*. Previous books include descriptive bibliographies of the work of William Everson and Karl Shapiro, *Earth Poetry: William Everson's Selected Essays and Interviews* (1980), and *Benchmark and Blaze: The Emergence of William Everson* (1979).